WILD PLUM CAFÉ

By Gretchen Butler

STARTING OVER:
*Tales of Homesteading
in Northern California's
Backcountry*

Gretchen Butler

Helen Verne Press

Front, back covers and artwork by Gretchen Butler
Graphic design by Gretchen Butler and Stephanie Endsley
Author photo by Jim Butler
Photo of water tanks, page 126, by Roger Butler
Photo of yurt construction group, page 133, by Jerry Taylor
Other photos by Gretchen Butler

Helen Verne Press
canyonstudio@gretchenbutler.com

Printed in the United States
by BookMobile

For my mother, Helen Verne, who yearned for mountains, forests, ferns, and green meadows when we lived in the dry hills of Southern California. She created a mini-mountain by shoveling dirt over a large, upside down sink basin. My dad called it Mt. Helena. She planted a row of drought tolerant cypress and made campfires, which we gathered round for songs and stories.

I am amazed that I'm living her long ago dream.

Contents

Acknowledgments:

Acknowledgment is made to the following publications in which some of these stories first appeared: *Redwood Coast Review, Russian River Times, MEMOIR (and.)*

Thank you, Amber Coverdale Sumrall, for your enthusiastic support and coaching on the use of precise language. Encouragement and guidance from Steve Smith, Sue Ritter-Splain, Julie Steinbach, Candida Lawrence are much appreciated. Greg Haynes launched me into the technical phase of the book when he loaned me *InDesign for Dummies* and gave my first tutorial in page layout. Stephanie Endsley and Sarah Dolinar rescued me when I was at my wit's end with computer skills, which started out significantly below the expections of commercial manuals. Stephanie's collaboration with font and format was delightful. Special thanks to friends who encouraged me to write the original Rancho Reports. Without them, I would not have written anything.

Our family and many friends helped us start over. My daughter, Jo McGarigle, Jim's brother, Roger Butler, along with Jerry Taylor, Rebecca Rollins, Brian and Sarah Dolinar, Beth Bennett, Dan Merritt, Dave Carr, Steve and Bonnie Chase set up the yurt and campsite under the Plum Tree Café. Shortly after the *Grand Prix* wild fire, assistance was given by Claremont Friends, the Gypsy Sisters, the Red Cross, Claremont Lion's Club, FEMA, Joan Hawthorne, the Bistline-Butler clan, and Buddhist monks, in their saffron robes, who walked to the end of our black, charred canyon, then personally handed each canyon family $500.

Jim and I are grateful to other thoughtful friends: Catherine Rojas and her husband met us at 6 a.m. the morning after the fire. Quilts, tools, baskets of food, gift cards and other donations were given by my daughter Jennifer McGarigle, Danny Bercu, Marla Collins, Jan Wheatcroft, B Amore, Joel and Theresa Houtman, Karen Chapman, Annabelle Whiting, Janet Sage, David Brodahl, Alicyn Goughnour, Jan Piacentine, Judy Dodd, Dee Cole, Deborah and Peter Hewitt, Jack Salter, Warren and Viesca Riner, Maria Costa, Gary Panovich, John and June Cullen, Ann Wilcox, Ron and Joan Arias, Vickie Monegan, Hitomi Yamamuro, Davetta Williams, Debbie Steiner, Susan Faye, Charlene Kreuger, Judy and Mark Hein. Anne Seltzer, my artist confidante, gave me the blank book with the beat-up, black cover where I scribbled this list.

Venus Rising

When he chooses the only road not on the national forest map, she stifles apprehension.

Campground comfort vanishes in dust. He investigates logging practices,

seeks solitude and panoramic vistas. She wears a whistle to scare bears.

He says, bears stay near campgrounds. He plays with bats at dusk,

tosses pebbles up as they dart and swerve.

She's lost in tree shadows 100-feet high.

He inhales their butter rum bark.

When a bright light intrudes

like a flashlight beam,

she's startled.

He says,

it's Venus rising.

She is
comforted
when she discovers
the footstep thuds
are pine cones falling on
the carpet of forest duff.

She unloads fears that were stuffed
in her backpack and they are crazed
with laughter as stars and nebulae light up.

In the middle of the night, she unzips the tent door,
steps outside, sits by herself in the clearing.

She and he and the Milky Way are embraced
by silhouetted tree beings.
She listens
to
their pine-songs.

PALMER CANYON

Against the advice of almost all my friends and family, I purchased a crooked house in a secluded canyon at the end of a dirt road. The foot bridge across the creek led to trails throughout chaparral foothills with an abundance of wildlife. In the other direction, I was 15 minutes from the school where I taught and six minutes from Claremont, a college town with concerts, lectures and fine restaurants.

The ancient oak holding a treehouse balcony above a year-round creek enchanted me and helped speed my recovery from divorce. Living near flowing water enhanced my daily awareness of the natural world and my place in it. The trickle in summer, the roar during winter storms and other fluctuations of flowing water helped me to become calm as I sorted through

1

life's perplexing dilemmas. As a teacher, it was easy to love students while helping them improve skills. As an activist for peace and justice, reconciliation was more difficult. In the canyon, I felt peaceful. These benefits easily outweighed the risks of living in a flood plain and wildfire zone. I accepted the possibility of disaster, but didn't worry much.

We were a cluster of independent, diverse and eccentric folks. Since we were beyond the city limits, we took responsibility for road and creek maintenance, and we took care of each other. When storms deluged the creek and flooded the crossing, I would park on a downstream high spot after work. In blustery, cold rains, Scott, our canyon's stalwart, ever-helpful giant, made sure each person got across. He lifted me up, carried me through a strong current and set me safely on the upper bank.

Two years after moving there, I met Jim and introduced him to the canyon. One night he came to visit and stayed for seven. In the midst of this heady affair, which resulted in marriage, he saw the dark, junky area below the house: his dream workshop.

Jim proceeded to jack up the house and rebuild its infrastructure, which became an artistic masterpiece. Above the two-foot deep foundation, he embedded a car engine block, bicycle parts, rusty tools, stones and bowling balls into a low wall. Cement foundation footings for salvaged telephone pole uprights were decorated with pennies, pebbles and marbles. The poles themselves had hooks for hanging coils of rope, chains, hammers and other tools.

Jim's shop became a gallery plastered with old signs: *You are expressly forbidden to trespass upon or pass over this property. Violators will be detained and held for the sheriff.* He placed *the Prepare to Unload sign over the toilet and the Please no singing, no dancing, no swearing-- This is a respectable house near our front doorway.*

Inside the shop, light shone through green, blue, brown and turquoise wine bottles which formed the outer wall between the poles. Jim fashioned an iron wagon wheel into a window. The workshop doorway and pumphouse shed were shingled with tin can lids, which turned rusty brown as they weathered.

He built a deck and picnic table over the creek, where we had dinner parties with lanterns, crickets, music and magic shows. When we installed new roofing visible from our upstairs bedroom window, we decorated the tarred seams with blue sparkles that glinted in moonlight. We were entertained by acorns dropping and rolling down in varying rhythms on the roof in the fall. Winter storms brought high water and huge boulders careening down the creek channel. In spring, I hung laundry on the treehouse railing and in summer we napped and nestled among cool leaves with hidden nests.

We explored the hills and followed the creek up past three waterfalls to its source, which was an inconspicuous seeping, wet spot in sand. We observed habits of owls and other birds, small creatures, insects and how they were affected by cycles of trees, vegetation and water. For 13 years, moonlight hikes and mountain bike rides through the hills helped balance our work routines. When I turned 60 and graduated from 24 years of teaching, we paid off our mortgage. We would live simply and be artists.

Sweet Spot

Before we lose our poems
and give up gathering
fresh yucca blossoms for soup,
while our pockets are crammed
with special pebbles, lupine seeds
and directions for cooking habanero chilies,
we hike downhill at dawn.

Moon sinks below shadows
as sun rises.
Owls glide to roost; wild oats glisten.
Fragrance of sage funnels through
the canyon's sweet spot.

Petals of the last blooming yucca
strew the road.
You place me under a dried stalk,
shake last year's pods.
Ten thousand shiny black seeds
rattle in rhythm—
falling
lighter than raindrops,
heavier than feathers.

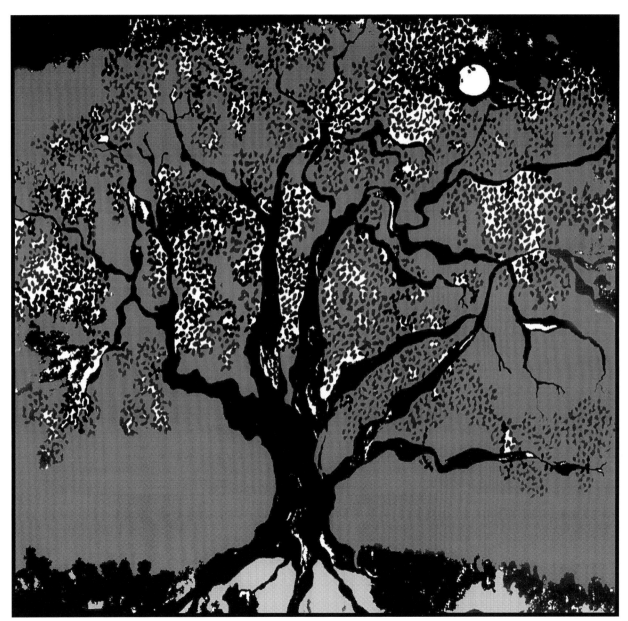

WILD FIRE

Even now, when I fully appreciate the outcome of the Oct. '03 *Grand Prix* wild fire that raged through 59,448 acres in Southern California, I'd rather not open the black smudged journal. Experiencing the fire and its aftermath is the beginning of our story, but I have been procrastinating thinking about it, writing about it. I'd much rather be digging, weeding, kneading bread or tackling a dozen other projects.

Most pages are blank. I have compulsively written in a journal since the 5th grade, but during this life-changing experience, I couldn't stand to do more than scribble notes and lists.

With binoculars, Jim studied the speck of light on the first day of the arsonist's blaze. As the Santa Ana winds picked up, he became more apprehensive. On the fifth day, I called a friend

6

three towns away and she said the nearby foothills were still safe. It seemed like a long, long distance away. In addition, the fire was on the other side of the large, dry river wash and dam. Moreover, our canyon is deep and fire does not go downhill; it tends to jump canyons. Homes have been here for a hundred years and more.

We were in bed when a canyon neighbor on the main road called at 10:20 p.m. to see if we wanted to hike up the mountain and watch. *Grand Prix* had jumped both the river wash and paved road. Our nearest hill tops glowed hot pink. We started packing and escaped twenty minutes later.

What I took:
  Important papers box, address book.
  Twenty framed, wrapped paintings ready for the upcoming sale and a large work in progress.
  Pillowcases of photo albums.

What Jim took:
  Computer equipment with art files and records.
  His carving that had begun as a 4-inch solid block of walnut. After 50 or more hours whitling with exact-o knives, Jim created a wooden "basket" that appeared to be carefully woven. By chance, it caught his eye and fit into his shirt pocket.
  Two of his many African drums.
  Our dog.
  The memory of his last look inside his work shop.

Jim's son, John, rushed up to help, but we were in such a hurry that we left with two empty trucks.

At midnight, neighbors and friends were with us amidst ferocious swirls of smoke, leaves, ash. Rotating red police lights dramatized explosions that spewed incredibly high flames. Ancient oaks and our gardens were gone, disintegrated as fire storms scoured the canyon back and forth four times. Fire engines on the freeway had raced 100 mph Santa Ana winds and flames to reach our area--and lost.

Friends took us to their home. The smell of ash permeated the town. I stared at orange, glowing foothills from the window; even though it was closed, we smelled fire. For many nights, I was held hostage by what I wished I had done that night and before.

What I wished I could have taken in the empty truck bed, but did not because my heart was pounding, because flames and embers were closing in on our long, one-way box canyon drive:

Jim's black Ecuadorian hat.

A set of hand-made dishes—each one different.

Jim's hand-carved chess set.

My daughter's whimsical drawing of our tree-house home perched on a canyon ledge. Jim's son's large, precise paprika can art.

Eighty per cent of my own art. (I especially miss the large abstract landscape, *Cosmic Seas,* evocative of stars and shooting stars falling, trailing above and below seas with layered

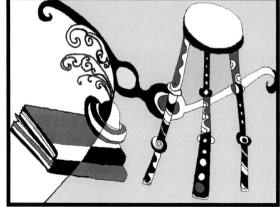

depths. Stare at those stars long enough and you could see them moving. After working on this piece outside all day, the first fall rains contributed magical, dripping runs of paint that I never would have thought of--perhaps they were a distant mountain connecting earth, and seas with the Milky Way and beyond.)

Hand-painted party stools.

Clothes from Guatemala and necklaces with beads from around the world made by a friend.

Antique furniture, Jim's refinished old rocker and the old seaman's chest full of vintage dress ups, hats, masks.

My joke box file, collected since fifth grade.

8

Jim's whimsical sculptures made from wood and rust.

The Tibetan brass "singing" bowl, a gift from a friend.
Jim's foreign currency collection.
His boxes of photos and mementos--birth bracelet and baby shoes, drawings from early childhood.
Special collections of early readers for grandchildren not yet born.
Hand-made fabrics and laces for gifts.

At the last minute, I could have grabbed at least one of these items. Or a month before, we could have purchased more expensive fire insurance instead of minimizing our budget. Even then, though, I never regretted having taken the risk of living there. I would do it all over again. Jim agreed.

I escaped from one of the dozens of community meetings one evening, and walked up the blackened canyon to our ghost house and enormous phantom oak. My tears, screams, wailing were swallowed up by a silent, moonless night.

No matter how helpful your community, friends and family are, no matter how many times you think *within chaos are seeds of opportunity* or *one door closes and another opens,* when you are grieving, nothing helps.

Three Days Later

Skeleton oaks: burned widow-maker branches fallen,
charred tree bones claw and scratch the sky.

Chimneys tower over rubble.
Inside her three-story phantom home,
a woman sifts through ashes
searching for treasures no matter how minute.

On our home-site promontory over
what used to be a creek, my heart cracks.
Invisible: upright piano from childhood,
Peruvian weavings, antique furniture.
My feet crunch my favorite shady green plates,
Grandma's blue platter and gold-rimmed wine glasses;
I'm losing my balance on unique hand-thrown bowls.
Too bad I'm crazy for dishes.
I recognize books, each bright white page is distinct.
They collapse in the poof of a touch.
Inhaled through a bandana mask, my history is toxic.

The creek's chock full of junk;
upside down bathtub, bedsprings.
The refrigerator had been chilling 150 tulip bulbs
before it was blown sky high
by exploding oxygen and acetylene tanks.
In Jim's wine bottle wall, 300 glass necks drop.

Sharp, gray shards cut our shoe soles.
Polluted sky seems like dusk, but it is only noon.
I want only one thing: to breathe clean air.

AFTER THE FIRE

We met frequently with our displaced canyon neighbors. Many were crazed with raging anger and grief, which they held onto as they demanded retribution from local, state and federal entities. They would spend months and years hoping to restore their canyon lives. Legal conflict and snarls with city and county agencies have still not been resolved. Six years later, no one has yet been able to rebuild.

After the fire, friends were generous. One couple shared their home with us for a month. Others offered house-sitting opportunities, household items and tools. The morning after, my Gypsy Sister artist friends delivered a selection of clothes that fit. (They are now almost worn out and I still love wearing them.)

Later, a friend met us in the canyon to help us retrieve Jim's treasured (non functional) fire hydrant, old chains and metal parts of shovels, rakes, and hoes. The young man, who lives in the city but explores wild territories, impulsively gave his hunting knife, which I have used for slicing everything from tomatoes to haunch of wild boar.

We, as recipients, also learned that to receive is to give. We were not accustomed to so many gifts. People wanted to help and our hearts received their goodwill. Sometimes, though, it was a challenge to graciously accept donations. I ended up distributing many bags of items to places where they were needed.

The shock of the fire and subsequent weeks of preparation for nine holiday art shows were dwarfed by my father's sudden illness. We tracked his cancer through all the medical hoops. He was cheerful, funny, perceptive, sensitive. He made each person in his presence feel special. A few weeks later, "The Old Gent" was gone.

After a period of mourning and caring for my parents' home, which was to be sold, we dreamed up eleven attributes of what we wanted in a new location. We hoped the new community would have a telephone book no thicker than a comic book and our house would be in the sun with a view of natural surroundings.

We had no desire for anything other than necessary possessions. We had sharp pangs when missing items gone up in smoke, but no interest in acquiring new ones. The loss of Jim's many, carefully preserved collections----foreign coins, photos, scientific magazines, the complete works of Mark Twain and other favorite authors--was liberating. He was released from his penchant to steal old, rusty signs and since then has not started any new collections. He lived with the mantra of the *Prajñaparamita Sutra:* "Gone, gone. All gone. Gone to the far shore. Enlightenment. WHOOPIE!"

I was in the simple moment for awhile. Four months after losing our home, my fast from wanting possessions was broken when we roamed Waddell Creek, one of our favorite beaches. For the first time since the fire, I wanted to have something: a few small, smooth dark rocks.

12

13

Top of the Pass

Strong wind
rushes through me and
I can't stop grinning.
Memories
of fire and destruction,
illness and death
will be with me
wherever I go,
but at this moment
they are on the other side
of the mountain.

Released by Lady Chance,
I'm headed out
onto the open Central Valley
and will follow a road that
weaves among
hill sculptures,
shadowy curves,
russet furrows,
fields and beyond to
a wild place
embraced
by gnarled oaks,
the sweetest spot.

BEAST

Within three days of our arrival in the ranch lands, three neighbors stop in the road to chat. Each one warns us: "You know, there are wild animals out here—rattlers, mountain lions and pigs. Watch out--and don't go out alone at dawn or dusk."

We plan to live outdoors during the summer. I thought I would enjoy this, but in less than a week, I'm nearly ready to divorce camping because of insomnia. Trapped in my mummy bag, I am too hot, too cold, too hungry at two a.m. Although I lay on three camping mattresses, uneven ground is ruining my back. Foxtails are in my socks, pine needles in my underwear. After five

16

nights of little sleep, perceptions are askew. Frazzled and haggard by day, I'm afraid at night.

In the wee hours of the sixth night, sounds bolt out of a fog suffused with eerie, waning moonlight. Fierce rooting and rustling, groaning, and loud exhalations from an enormous beast fill the night. A cow attacked by a lion in a boggy ravine? Or a wild hog with glowing eyes and razor-sharp tusks ripping up the meadow of daisies? The neighbor had said, "Pigs completely destroy whatever is in their path. Get out of their way. Nothing you can do—unless you have a rifle."

Soon the sounds of snorting and crashing through brush and branches come from the wild plum tree area where my outdoor kitchen shelves are lashed to the trunk. Any minute the wash stand on the flimsy cart and the cardtable with a stack of dishes will crash. But the snorting recedes through the brush and mist and I don't awaken my exhausted husband.

I lie awake eating nuts and chocolate chips while remembering the previous night's stunning Milky Way, which stretched as far as the eye could see. The heavens are not peaceful: super nova explosions, dwarf stars swallowed by black holes, death and birth on a mega scale are facts to accept. It doesn't bother me that 96% of Dark Matter and Dark Energy baffle our scientists. Or that I am an insignificant speck in an apparently impersonal, mysterious universe. In fact, I love it.

A month before, we had learned that this land was for sale and hiked up this hill for the first time. The view across the long valley took our breath away. Well, we were already out of breath from the climb. We felt ourselves open out beyond sloping meadows and green firs, bays, maples that cover the ridges. We could not see a single house or road. No telephone or electric poles. The only sound was wind rushing through the boughs. It took ten minutes to decide to make this our home.

This quick, clear decision was surprising because we are in our sixties. Our original plan was to find a fixer-upper on the outskirts of a small town. We thought we might find a cottage with a small garden plot that had already been rototilled.

The night before climbing up this hill for the first time, we stayed with old friends on an adjacent ranch. When Jim saw the wind generator, solar panels, ingenious use of building materials and yurts, his mind started churning. I didn't sleep that night, either. No, no, not for me, I thought. I didn't want to work that hard to exist, to be two hours from movies, restaurants and cultural events, to be far from help should we be injured or ill.

But during our search for a cottage near town, we discovered that our limited resources were not enough. This turned out to be fortuitous because we ended up crazy in love with this land. There was no house or shelter, but a reliable spring and the underground telephone cable made us feel confident. Later, we learned how—many years ago—each of our neighbors felt when they found their land. One said, "On my first visit, I decided I would do anything to live here."

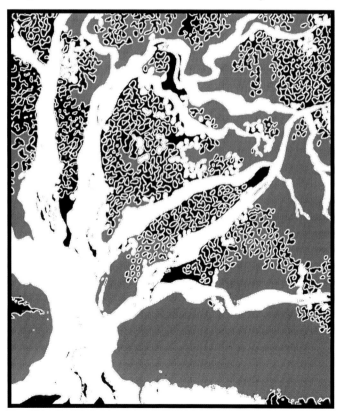

Our decision was like that. The long view across the southwest, the space lit by dawn and surrounded by ancient oaks, the waving grasses—all felt like home.

Previous losses and the recent death of my father gave me a renewed appreciation for mortality and for living fully. I did not want to miss this opportunity to learn and be part of a beautiful place which made me feel both excited and peaceful. We felt reconnected with the whole shebang and surrendered to the consequences: the long, tortuous drive to town, inconveniences and discomforts of living off the grid, the absence of close friends.

Our friends and relatives were alarmed that we would take such risks at our age. I dismissed their concerns and advice.

Danger is everywhere. Hundred car pile-ups on Hwy. 99, West Nile virus caught from a mosquito in the backyard, broken bones from falling into a manicured rose garden. Earthquakes, muggings in upscale malls, or black widows or scorpions in your bed.

These thoughts whirl through my mind as I force myself to breathe and relax inside the flimsy tent. Gradually, I become less afraid of what's out there. At this moment, I am snug and safe.

At dawn, I creep along the narrow path lined with damp grasses as tall as I am. The plum tree kitchen is intact. Jim joins me for coffee in our sunny breakfast spot. Even after two cups, he doesn't buy my account of the beast. He says, "We're lucky those pigs didn't snuff up all the coffee and pierce the canned tomato sauce with one of their seven tusks!"

A few days later, we meet a young rancher in his pick-up. He stops in the road and introduces himself. As the dust settles, I ask him about The Beast. He listens to my tale and especially to my loud rendition of Beast noise, then concludes, "Well, Ma'am, that Beast was a buck in rut. He was doin' the dosey doe, Ma'am. That's as nice as I can put it. The dosey doe."

Jim's List

Cargo container for emergency shelter and storage of furniture from my parents' home.

Water system: install a 2,500-gallon tank up the hill, pipes that run downhill to a water faucet near our campsite. Commercial water delivery to the main tank this first season.

Propane generator rented to run power tools.

Weed whack tall grass in a large circle for the yurt. Level cement block footings for yurt floor.

Trenches for water, telephone and power lines.

Solar panels, batteries, back up propane generator.

Finish To Do List before the rainy season--about five months.

My List

Shelves for storing food near the camp stove and ice boxes.

An outhouse. (It was more "out" than house. Our hole in a box had a smooth, oak seat and was painted to blend in with golden grsses and forest greenery. Toilet paper and an appropriate sonnet written by one of our visitors were in an attractive box near a pot of lime and wild flowers in a vase. The view of the glen and surrounding forest with deer and rabbits was exhilarating. Even after we had indoor facilities, Jim used this throne, which he dubbed the Summer Palace.)

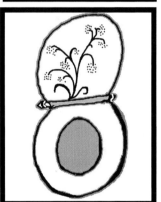

A simple bed with an air mattress and nine blankets that don't drag on the ground. (Sleeping outside was far more comfortable and beautiful than in the tent.)

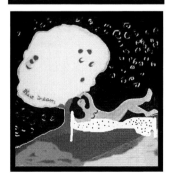

Rancho Report: June 2004

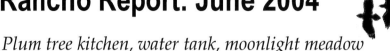

Plum tree kitchen, water tank, moonlight meadow

Jim's brother, my daughter and two friends helped us unpack and set up camp. We wanted to have a light footprint on this land, but in one short day we humans had beaten a prominent path through the meadow grasses. After we unloaded the U-Haul, our stuff was everywhere.

Each nearby tree is a room in our outdoor house. Jim's workshop tools lean against a pine, art frames and paint supplies encircle a eucalyptus. The new oak toilet seat and plywood for the "Summer Palace" are under the bay. My kitchen is under the wild plum.

My mother, who was an interior decorator, would appreciate this kitchen with its pine-needle carpet that needs no vacuuming and the "window" view of oak trees on the sunny knoll. I remember how pleased she was in the 50's to have new, matching chests and bookshelves. The bedroom ensemble she so carefully dusted will be outside next to the camp stove for five months or more. Rain or shine. Her bookshelves, lashed to the wild plum, hold her dishes. A bouquet of wild flowers is next to canned goods, kalamata olives, and marinated tomatoes.

While dishwashing, I feel like I'm playing house. The plastic box sink is on my mom's metal rolling cart with its useless electric plug.

Waist-high grasses, millions of small daisies and wild fennel with a cocoon are before me. The outdoor home is delightful now, but will I have a mess when plums ripen and fall?

Jim is working on the water system. He and his buddy Archimedes jockey the giant nine-foot high green tank into place. Even I am able to help move it. With one finger I press my end of the long board, which is on a fulcrum. The other end is under the tank, which moves inch by inch.

After we install pipes that will carry water from the tank in the high meadow down to our summer site, we will have 2,500 gallons delivered. We hope that will hold out until we are able to pump from the spring, which will depend on electricity from the solar panels.

Tonight, Jim, Roger (his brother) and I will play Scrabble by full moonlight. We gather around the card table with a blue and white checked oilcloth. The table with a vase of daisies is surrounded by a meadow of daisies, which is a larger bouquet. In moonlight, the tall grasses are illuminated and become a magic curtain which makes me feel safe. Night birds with soft, fluttering conversations guide us to bed before we fall asleep in our chairs and mess up the game board.

Note on communication: the underground phone line surfaces out in the field. Jim leans on a fallen log and holds the laptop so that we can receive email. We can't send messages yet, though. My dad's old dial phone is hooked up, but there's no answering machine. Please let it ring 20 times so we have a chance to run out there. Our cell phone will take messages, but it may be days before I am somewhere with reception and am able to harvest them. The post office ladies hold mail for us until we are able to install a mailbox on the main road.

Love,
Gretchen and Jim

Jim's Meditation

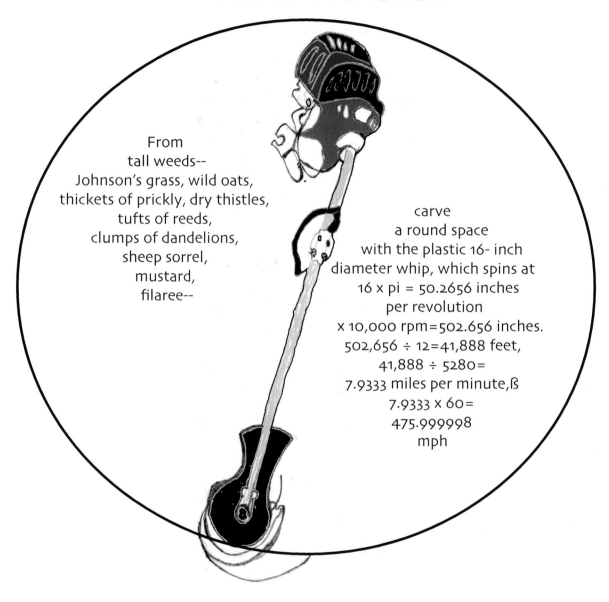

From
tall weeds--
Johnson's grass, wild oats,
thickets of prickly, dry thistles,
tufts of reeds,
clumps of dandelions,
sheep sorrel,
mustard,
filaree--

carve
a round space
with the plastic 16- inch
diameter whip, which spins at
16 x pi = 50.2656 inches
per revolution
x 10,000 rpm=502.656 inches.
502,656 ÷ 12=41,888 feet,
41,888 ÷ 5280=
7.9333 miles per minute,ß
7.9333 x 60=
475.999998
mph

YURT RAISING

The yurt crates are twice the width of the hydraulic lift on the delivery truck. Jim tells Salvador, the driver, *"Lentamente como un zopilote no mas"* (Go slowly like a buzzard) as he begins to lower the largest package with the dome. Balancing on the edge of the tailgate, Jim leverages with the pry bar as we position two hand trucks on the ground. He nudges the box left, then straight as Roger pushes. My heart is pounding, but it doesn't crash off the side. They ease the lift down, slide the cargo onto the receiving hand trucks. I peek inside: wood doors, rafters, supports, high tech shiny insulation and dark green plastic walls, plexi-glass dome and a hefty steel cable which counters the outward thrust of the rafters.

Without any previous plans, five friends with tents arrive the next day. We put up the platform, walls and roof in a few days. Door fittings and floor finishing take longer.

SPRING

While Jim installs pipes and a 2,500 gallon tank, one of my jobs is filling and carrying jugs of water for garden, bathing and dishes from the spring. I feel like Alice as I make my way through wonderland grasses tall as I am. This is curiously different from my Southern California lifestyle. For decades, a rushing whirlwind of activities, work routines, family dramas and artistic endeavors propelled me along.

After the fire, I twisted my knee in my first yoga class, which was my first attempt to do something healthy for myself. During the opening, easiest exercise—the Child's Pose—my knee completely gave way and soon I could scarcely walk.

This was the same month when I took time for a cup of tea at a friend's home where we were about to begin house-sitting. Wanting a moment of comfort and solitude, I picked out the perfect hand-painted cup for my favorite tea. The moment I sat down, the full cup jumped out of my hand. Now both halves are amongst my garden flowers.

By the time we arrived on our land, I had weaned myself from painkillers, but had difficulty walking on uneven terrain. With a weed-whacker Jim carved a trail down the meadow slope, past wild raspberries covering a fallen log, an ideal home for a rattler. Slowly trudging up and downhill was effective therapy for my knee and it has not bothered me since.

On one of those first trips, I realized that I'd better train myself to be alert to the presence of animals and snakes camouflaged in forest shadows and deep grass. A minute after I tilted the large brim of my sunhat up to pay better attention, I stepped on the tail of a brown snake on the shady path. He was my first creature teacher with this rule: *watch where you step.*

At dusk Jim and I tramped through the lower meadow and discovered a gorgeous king snake with black and white bands. He is helpful (from my point of view) because he preys on rattlers, but his presence increased my rattler apprehension.

We had entered the bay forest—no path amidst twigs, dead leaves and tree detritus. If there were rattlers, they'd be invisible until it was too late. We managed to remain unharmed by shuffling through the forest duff until we met up with the spring path.

My water fetching routine entails carrying eight empty plastic jugs downhill and two full jugs uphill. Most days, I welcome cool shade and perch on a boulder in the creek, fed by clear, pure water that trickles from heavy, black muck under the giant bay laurel. Filling each gallon jug takes seven minutes.

Hans Arp, a poet-artist from the DaDa cultural movement after WWI, noted that there are two clocks: one from swallows for the fast days, one from turtles for the slow ones. Both clocks tick away during my visits to the spring. My busy, practical mind figures out dinner menus as I position jars of mustard, salsa, mayonaise and a bottle of chardonnay in the small, cool pool. I plan all the ways I will "spend" the water I carry up.

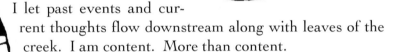

Holding the jug under the trickle and listening to the tones of rising water slow me down. Mossy rocks glow chartreuse for the few minutes it takes the sun to pass over them, and enormous sword ferns become backlit. Rivulet patterns in mud are like miniature versions of the Grand Canyon.

I let past events and current thoughts flow downstream along with leaves of the creek. I am content. More than content.

WILD PLUM CAFÉ

I painted *Wild Plum Café* while sitting beneath squawking stellar jays and chattering acorn woodpeckers. Their chirps crescendoed into mayhem and they rushed off in a flurry when the raven landed with his harsh barking call. This glossy, bossy bird picked, pecked and dropped discarded plums on my head while I painted him.

Our wild plum most likely sprouted from a bird dropping fifty years ago. Our neighbor said these trees were introduced by the government throughout the area to provide food during The Depression. Ever since, in late June and July, abundant fruit has attracted birds and squirrels by day, possums and raccoons by night.

There are plenty of plums for all of us and I became a slave to picking the round, sticky cherry-sized fruit from a ladder and off the ground. I boiled five batches of jam on the camp stove, gave them to the post office women or anyone who happened to come down the road.

During Plum Drop, I raked up pits, skins, dirt and leaves every day, but even so, our mutt, Riley, became matted with gummy, black plum parts. Normally, he had a long-haired, golden coat, but now he wore large patches of brown-black plaster. Jim cut off the worst parts, which were embedded with wild carrot burrs.

The tree's generous canopy shaded our kitchen/dining room, where recently we had our first dinner party with a neighboring family that lives half a mile away. Jesús and Pat brought their daughter, Merlín which means aquamarine in Spanish as well as magician and hawk in English. Her younger, eight year old brother with shoulder length hair was not mistaken for girl because he introduced himself as Donald Jesús Velasquez Greer with confidence. He said we could call him "Sito," the nick name for Jesusito.

They especially liked the solar oven made from a plywood box insulated with an old towel and tinfoil. The metal reflectors and a plexi-glass cover resting on two nails heat the box up to 250 degrees, which is hot enough to bake pioneer cookies if you leave them in two hours. The cookies, made without a recipe and without traditional ingredients, were oatmeal dough blobs with chocolate chips and nuts.

We ate all the cookies after the meal, which started with an appetizer of crackers with olive tapanade garnished with johnny-jump up flowers, followed by pasta with sundried marinated tomatoes, basil and wild salmon from a can. After we chatted into the evening, the family packed themselves and the two kids' bikes onto the four-wheeler and roared up the hill.

I collected dirty dishes as Jim started the nightly routine: position the car so that he could connect the blow-up mattress cord into the inverter, which plugged into the cigarette lighter. The mattress, which had a mysterious leak, remained inflated all night only if we went to this trouble. After inflating the mattress, Jim disconnected all the cords and parked the car, which was on a slight slope. It was late. He was tired, and inadvertently, did not put on the parking brake on all the way.

We froze as we watched the car slowly, invincibly pick up speed and crash into the wild plum tree and kitchen. Collapsing, distorting cupboards and shelves seemed to break apart in slow motion. We saw jars, dishes, cans and pots take long minutes to fly uphill and down. Mexican glass and handmade ceramic bowls were smashed with tinkles of falling shards. A few dishes —the ones that I did not care for—were in perfect condition.

Shocked, angry, and exhausted, we shook our heads and went to bed. The tree trunk stopped the car so that it didn't careen down the embankment, but Jim felt terrible. I relived the sounds of the crash a hundred times that night.

By the next evening, we had everything picked up, Jim refashioned the kitchen and I accepted the loss of dishes, which was nothing compared to losing everything in the fire. With my kitchen intact, I felt secure. I didn't understand much about any of the projects we were attempting. I only knew about cooking.

We told Jesús's family about the crash. Our disbelief, the cacophany of square shelves becoming parallelograms, cans and dishes crowding, crushing, rolling, sliding, flying, descending, breaking to bits: we couldn't stop laughing.

31

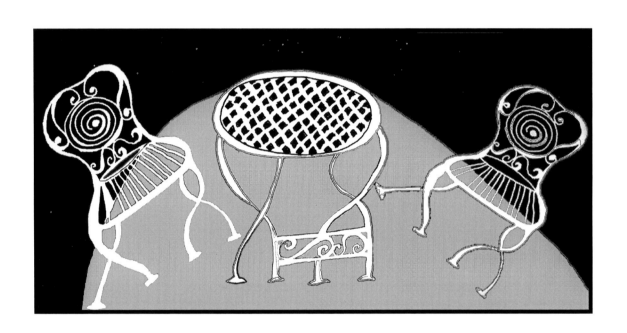

Camping Dinners

Pears with gorgonzola cheese, walnuts, romaine lettuce with vinaigrette; fried yam slices with oregano and garlic

Penne with 14 garlic cloves in arrabiata red sauce, basil and carrots; green salad with oranges

Corn on the cob dipped in olive oil with chopped parsley, hot pepper flakes, grated pecorino cheese; potato salad with hard boiled egg, cucumber slices, diced green onion

Omelette with basil, feta cheese, green onions; thick pancakes with wild plum syrup

Cherry tomatoes in vinaigrette; savory bean soup cooked in solar oven, crackers and wild plum jam

Soup with marinated artichoke hearts, carrots, onions, potatoes, seasonings; toasty pan-fried wheat bread

Baby red potatoes, rosemary, onion, marinated sundried tomatoes; mango, jicama with lemon juice and grated nutmeg

Avocado, refried beans with tortilla chips on lettuce, kalamata olives, brown rice, apple slices

Tortilla wrap falafel (from a mix) and chopped tomatoes, green onion, cucumber; black bean, corn, tomato salad

F & A BLUES

We've had open trenches with mounds of red and black earth waiting for cables, wires, pipes for many weeks. It might be another three months before I have a real stove or refrigerator. I feel helpless. We're both running scared because winter's around the corner. We're not ready. Soon we'll move into the yurt, but our wood stove has not arrived and we need to stack and keep future fire wood dry under tarps. The Power House must be roofed so that it is snug, ventilated and protected on the exterior. For this season, tarpaper will have to do.

Last week, I had the Fear and Anxiety Blues. I was disappointed that our local solar experts had not yet received the parts for our electrical system. I should have been glad that we are on back order because Germany has purchased huge shipments of solar panels to revolutionize its public power system, but I was off balance: my expectations were out of sync with reality.

34

My ten-pound supply of chocolate chips was consumed, I was annoyed with limited food storage--blocks of ice melt in three days. When the camp stove propane canister ran out while the multi-grain cranberry pan bread was half-cooked, I got crabby. Probably, when I can finally cook indoors, I'll wish I were outside under the wild plum again. I'll miss the sweet incense of leaves and pine needles that fall into the Coleman burner flames.

Jim took me out to dinner (the nearest restaurant is 45 minutes away) and I came back no longer grim, no longer completely focused on inconveniences and dashed hopes. When I returned from the evening of dining on the coast, I was able to look in both directions instead of being stuck in a zoom lens close-up perspective. Now, I look one way and see dug up earth, holes, salvaged windows, doors, sinks, toilet, white, gray and black pipes, spools of cable, plywood, garden fencing, and one extra-long bathtub with grass growing all around it. In the other direction, golden hills, shady glens, gnarled oaks, birds and sky jazz me up and calm me down.

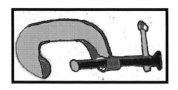

Tools

Hammers: claw, framing (smooth face and waffle) rubber mallet, maul, six lb. sledge

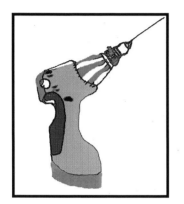

Saws: chop, skill, pole, saws-all, jig, rip, cross cut, table, chainsaw

Drills: cordless, right-angle, high-speed metal, hydraulic auger

Screwdrivers: Phillips, blade, square, slotted

Pliers: water pump, fencing, electrician, wirestripper, needle nose, dikes

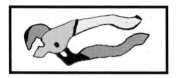

Wrenches: box, open end, adjustable, crescent, Stilson, monkey, pipe, rachet

Shovels: trenching, square-nose, scoop, trowel, spade

Levels: pipe, torpedo, line

Jacks: house, car, hydraulic, bottle, scissors

Bars: crow, digging, wonder, long handled breaker

Rakes: leaf, garden, bow

More: Come-along, loppers, jumper cables, C-clamp, plumb bob, torch, vise, snap line, pipe cutter, shim

Rancho Report: Sept. 2004

Yurt, Power House, Jim's music, kids and cats

Even on hot days, we enjoy natural air conditioning under the plum and pine trees. The hills are straw gold, the forests dusty and dry. Jim discovered that if you wet the brown, shriveled moss on a fallen branch with pee, it unfurls and becomes green. Fat acorn bullets bonk us on the head; the madrone's red bark is peeling off and sounds like trickling water.

We're learning all sorts of pioneer know-how, so maybe we're pulling out of what Jim calls BFI (brute force and ignorance.) I'm able to carry an ice box of water without sloshing, pollinate squash by jiggling the female blossoms, sprout seeds in a heat wave and use a come-along to help pull down large trees.

I have knee pads, buckles, goggles, nose filters and choose correct sandpaper grit for orbital sanding on the yurt floor. I know about dead nuts leveling, joists, trusses and gussets and how not to bother Jim with my fabulous suggestions on construction until he's had two cups of coffee in silence as the sun is coming up.

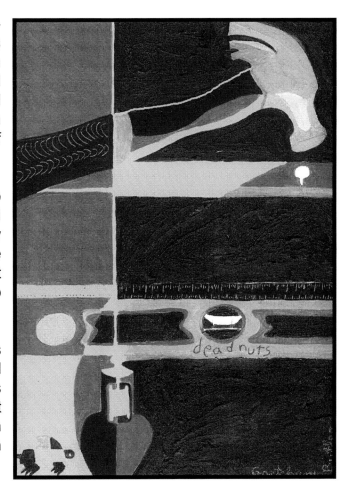

We have raised four walls of the 8'x8' Power House, which will hold the batteries and brains of the solar panel system. After Jim framed each wall on the ground, we lifted hundreds of pounds to a vertical position inch by inch. He maneuvered the crowbar while I stacked 2x4 blocks that held the wall until he constructed temporary diagonal braces between the wall frame and the ground. Guard rails kept the wall from slipping into the deep trench for electric wiring. While he measured right angles for joining the corners, I balanced the 300-pound vertical wall. I breathed heavily from fear of dropping it.

Jim is a champion pioneer at 60. He has arthritic aches and pains, but is remarkably spry. He jumps in and out of the pick up bed, explores steep ravines, hikes on the road at night by starlight. He sings more than he curses while he works. He knows all the Beatles' tunes and blues songs I've never heard before. He spontaneously transforms bottles and sticks into musical instruments; for example, he plays a cvc pipe as if it were a Tibetan prayer horn.

Our neighbor kids, Sito and Merlín, gave us two kittens, one gray and the other black. They no longer wrestle all night on top of us— they crawl under the covers, down to the bottom and are furry foot warmers.

Riley is tolerant when they rub against him, but he does not let them sleep with him. When they nestle next to him on his sleeping pad, he moves over. They continue to move and snuggle against him until he gives up altogether and sleeps on the ground.

We also find one of our *gatitos* asleep in an abalone shell or a bowl or the bathroom sink, which nests in tall grass. The rest of the time they scamper around the campsite and join us as we work.

Merlín and Sito help in many ways. They've become skilled at using the claw end of the hammer to yank nails out of wood scraps which can be recycled. They make concoctions for baking in the solar oven and form tortillas with a primitive wooden press. After racing around dirt piles and jumping over trenches, they play Yahtzee, dominoes and learn to do mind-reading tricks with cards.

Nights are balmy. Crickets provide a background chorus for pygmy owl conversations: soft, fluttering exchanges spiced with bursts in pitch and volume. Coyotes yap. Yips and yelps from the moms and kids escalate until old man coyote lets out a long, haunting howl. Suddenly, they hush up.

Jim is studying constellations, but I have a hard time keeping track of shifting specks of light that do not resemble their names. During the day, though, I can glance at the sun and tell the time within three minutes.

Winter storms are coming, but we'll be fine. After all, this isn't Alaska.

Love,
Gretchen and Jim

Jim's Songs

Honky Tonk Blues
I mean what I mean my boogie woogie country girl....
Rockin' Robin
Don't worry 'bout them dreams, they only in your head...
My Gal's a Corker
Take My Lips
Midnight on the Water
Frer a Jacque
Wishing my long lost lover would walk to me, talk to me....
Red Bird Sings
How Can I Live Without You
On the Road to Mandalay
The Harder They Come
Tennessee Waltz
Raven hair, ruby lips, sparks from her fingertips....
King Kamehaha
King of the Road
We are big rock singers, we got golden fingers....
Do Your Duty
Peter and the Wolf
Great Balls of Fire
Watch out where the huskies go and don't you eat that yellow snow....
The Walrus
Sargeant Pepper
It's a Long Day's Night
And your shoes keep walkin' back to me.....
Justine, Justine You Just Don't Treat Me Right
Ain't she sweet, see her walkin' down the street...
Yakity yak don't talk back.....
Johnny Too Bad

FIRST STORM

Before I have a chance to enjoy my afternoon snack of cashews and an apple, dark clouds and wind blow in, faster than anticipated. I teeter between crabbiness and wild laughter. Jim is grinning.

First task is to wrap our almost- finished Power House with the largest tarp. Tarpaper is on only one side and the roof vent pipe isn't up yet. We (mostly Jim) built this 8'x'8' treasure that houses the solar panels' brains and batteries, which must not get wet.

Jim is silhouetted on top of the shed roof as black clouds loom behind him, except when he's swallowed up in the billowing brown tarp. He is more wrapped than the building. I guide the lower edges while he wrestles to organize the flapping corners from above. We hoist long 2x4's to hold them down and he laces my clothesline through grommet holes all the way around and ties it snugly. The Power House is wrapped.

Our next job is to move and wrap a stack of plywood. We load and balance groups of four 4'x8' sheets onto the wheelbarrow. It's almost dark, raining lightly and I'm so hungry I have a hard time concentrating. Jim coaches me, "Slide it, Babycake, push, don't pull…"

We turn 90 and then 180 degrees with a precarious 8-foot wide load. After six stanzas of the wheelbarrow rotation routine I have the dance pattern down. No toppling.

By twilight and flashlight in a cold, windy rain, we fill the wheelbarrow with firewood and deliver it to the yurt. I grunt while climbing the high tree stump steps up to the doorway.

After the outside work is finished, comes the worst time. It is pitch-black and I have trouble finding the extra flashlight. Jim is in an outrageously cheerful mood as he hands me items for dinner from the outside ice chest: a freezing, sopping, leaking plastic bag with two carrots and a bottle of wine. I yell at him because he's dripping water on the new floor and then I throw the bag out the door. Also throw out the leaking propane canister from the camp stove. Can scarcely thread the new canister on with wet, cold fingers. Muddy dog, cats and humans puddle across the floor.

Jim asks for coffee—I hate making coffee at this hour! After he locates dry socks and after I spill the kitchen matches, he lights a candle.

I give him the last dry towel. Well, it's dry until I drag it through the dog water dish.

I sigh my own rain cloud of frustration. Loudly.

"Why are you moaning like this is the last straw?" he asks. "We did everything in time!"

"This *is* the last wet straw!"

"Shall we live in a condo?"

That shuts me up.

He spills the rest of the matches out of the damp box and starts the woodstove fire. The place warms up slowly because I must keep the door open to vent the camp stove while I quickly heat up dinner. I remember to take off my dad's knit neck scarf before the fringes catch on fire.

While I throw dinner together, he sits by the fire reading *The Decline and Fall of the Roman Empire* by candlelight, removing himself from me by six centuries.

At last, dinner: freshly picked zucchini, brown rice, onions, carrots. A glass of chardonnay lifts me out of my roiling cauldron. Chocolate chip pioneer cookies made without a recipe, without proper ingredients, without an oven — burned on one side, raw on the other. Delicious.

Thunder rolls, rain blasts the thin walls of the yurt. The fire crackles in warm light. It is exciting to be this close to the elements and yet feel secure.

My feet are cozy in fuzzy red socks and I beat the socks off Jim in Canasta.

Open doors:

crisp
oak
leaves

amber light

flutter,

settle on the floor.

I don't sweep for a week.

Rancho Report: Jan. 2005

Decorating the yurt, electricity, cooking, cutting firewood

Last night's Rip Snorter blasted us—rain squalls and 40 mph winds rammed into the yurt like football tacklers. Exhilarating entertainment—I was shrieking with each lightning bolt's thundering, booming crash and also from the suspense of our candlelit Canasta battle. Lots of wild cards in my hand.

The whole world glistens this morning. Oaks have put on their vibrant moss green sweaters outlined with gold; their branches and lacy twiglets sway. I dance in slow motion as two ravens glide in lazy circles. They are taking a break from their punctual, direct flight routine.

This feels like home now. Meadows, forests, birds and animals open our hearts each day. We get a kick out of being resourceful; accomplishments bring great pleasure. The yurt has colorful weavings and fabrics from around the world that hide the criss-cross wall lattice. Even on gray, rainy days, light from the plexi-glass dome makes the 24-foot diameter seem spacious and cheerful.

Since the last equinox report, everything I feared would happen has happened. We don't have an indoor bathroom or kitchen sink. However, my anticipatory anxiety was worse than the actual experience. When we have muddy, drippy times, I breathe deeply, take a tip from Islam and give thanks at least five times a day. Six squirrels scamper and jump through treetop pathways. Acorn woodpeckers always have something to squawk about. Their construction and food storage projects are finished, and I miss their rat-a-tat pecking.

Jim enjoys each day. He wakes up and exclaims, "We get to pull wires today!" or "The sun is coming up in the east—just the way I like it!" Every morning, he shovels mud that fills the infrastructure trenches. He says a meditative rhythm synchronizes with the physical one, making him feel like a steam shovel scooping, swiveling on giant ball bearings in one smooth motion. He also has the satisfaction of knowing his precious propane, electric and water lines are safely below ground and up to code.

November was unusually sunny, and our local contractor was able to roof the future Winter Bath House. This small structure now houses our little fridge, which is making ice cubes out of sunbeams. The solar panels provide electricity, which flows through wire to the Power House, where it's stored in batteries and converted to 110 volts.

When deciding where to place the solar panels four months ago, we refused to have them interrupt our view of the valley. Our contractor predicted that although we might not think the system aesthetically beautiful, we would change our definition of beauty when we enjoy the benefits. That is true. The solar panels' purple-blue elements sparkling in the sun are gorgeous.

We frequently check the indoor monitor, which shows how much battery power we have used. If cloudy skies diminish the daily charge rate, we minimize our use of electricity. We have the propane generator as a back up power source, but we try to avoid using it. Knowing how much juice is consumed by appliances and lightbulbs, we are satisfied to not waste electricity and limit our needs to what we have. It's like not overdrawing the bank account.

Electric lights and the fridge make life much easier. I especially appreciate Queen Amana, a 4-burner stove with an oven. Cinnamon rolls and baked cookies are a welcome change from pioneer pandowdies (burned on one side, raw on the other.) I am glad I have something delicious to share with a neighbor who brings a bouquet of daffodils.

Our first Netflix movie will arrive by mail, which we'll watch on the laptop computer. We're starved for movies, for other people's drama, for escape from Canasta battles.

When it's not raining, we rustle up wood stove fuel. Jim cuts a fallen oak with the chain saw, then splits it. He finds a tiny crack, sets the splitter spike into that perfect spot, whacks it with a big mallet. I load the wheelbarrow with logs and kindling, then stack them near the stove to dry out. I would probably be too sedentary if I weren't scared of being cold all day. This is much better than exercizing at a sweaty gym with no windows.

To celebrate New Year's, we hiked along deer trails that meander around hills and ravines. On every excursion, our dog and the gray cat join us as we discover new plants, niches, views. I especially enjoy these jaunts because snakes are hibernating.

We are now able to receive email and we welcome every form of communication.

Love,
Gretchen and Jim

BACK ROADS

Last night, coming home from a birthday party on the adjacent ranch, we saw familiar landscape in a new light. When there is no moon, car headlights reveal only foreground. Background: hills, ravines, swales, hundreds of acres of firs are deleted, become deep black. What is commonplace in daytime—grasses swaying and ancient oaks bent at odd angles—become spectacular surprises as we round each curve.

The CD played drum music from Mali. Village women were yelling and screaming with abandon. Along with the music, we were almost out of control as we fishtailed in mud and eased over ruts gushing with water. Although we were going slowly, it felt like we were on the edge of the earth. Better than the wildest ride at Magic Mountain.

In daylight, I tend to speed on dirt roads, especially after rain. On a straight stretch I recklessly get up to 25 mph, swerving around mud puddles. But mostly I have come to accept and appreciate the slow pace of one-lane, winding roads with steep embankments. Just as in life, we can't see very far ahead, so we might as well slow down, look around.

Each bend opens onto a new scene: an ancient lichen-laden fence leaning into the hilly slope of wild oats, a mini-waterfall crashing over boulders, redwood trees seven feet in diameter, nine vultures spreading their dewy wings to dry in morning sun. Nocturnal ringtail cat sightings are so rare that neighbors think we imagine them.

We have waited for enormous wild pigs to amble off the road and have found trucks stopped in the middle while the driver chases and captures a scampering wild piglet, his curly tail shiver-

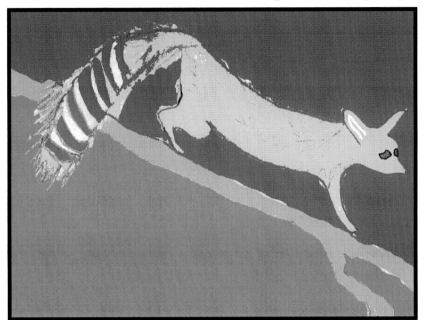

ing with terror. Deer bounce through meadows and over fences as if their legs were springs. Or a does waits quietly with her spotted fawn until we pass. Black angus cows also have the right of way; while a calf nurses, the mother chews her cud and placidly watches us.

My comfort zone has enlarged since first traversing these country roads. I used to shut my eyes, hold my breath, and hang on when Jim pulled over next to a ravine to let another car pass. There are few other cars—so it is an event when one comes along. Usually, the driver stops to chat in the middle of the road.

Some visitors have been so dizzy on the steep grades and hairpin curves that they've had to abandon their cars and walk. Or we have escorted them part of the way when they don't trust our map's landmarks such as *follow the creek, go left after the seventh cattle-guard, or turn right before the old truck.* We secretly gloat when 21st century GPS directions do not match the back roads.

In the fall, the carpet of golden maple leaves is so thick you would not know there was a road at all. We and our neighbors hope these roads always remain unmarked, unpaved.

On the main road we take to town, love notes on paper plates are tacked onto trees. *Amour de mi vida, I (heart-shape) you or Every day my love grows.* Further on, the tamale lady is on the side of the road. If she isn't there, she leaves a sign to tell you when she'll be back. The coffee shop's homemade sign says, *Honk if you want car service.* In spring, cherry vendors sell from their truck beds and colorful flags surround the guy who sells wind chimes.

Loving these back roads is part of the huge lifestyle change since we left Southern California. For us, sirens, stoplights, freeway jams, mad drivers, drivers talking on cell phones are a nightmare. We were surprised when Jim's sister's eyes grew wide as she described driving our back roads at night. She felt she was in a horror movie when her headlights flashed on waving grasses and oaks angling across the road.

It's About Time

Almost daffodil time,
Sometime, down time,
Prime time, keep time, 4/4 time,
Rock around the clock.

High time, chow time, thyme and sage,
Time-line, timely fashion, time is of the essence,
Deadline,
Procrastinate.

In the nick of time, just in time, on time,
Behind the times,
Time flies, *tempis fugit*,
 Waste time,
Time of the month.

Early,
This point in time,
Clock in, rush hour, minute hand,
Late.

Martime, Pacific Standard Greenwich Time,
Olden days,
Days of yore,
Prehistoric time,
Sidereal time,
Space-time continuum,
Pause,
Anon,
Now.

NO KITCHEN SINK BLUES

Yesterday, Jim was studying trees—noting which ones could become uprights for a workshop or shed or carport. It's no fun being a nag or nervous wreck about the kitchen sink, so I ask if those projects are on front or back burners.

"Oh, those are back burners," he says. "Your sink and back porch and bathroom are on front burners. There are a lot of burners, but only two speeds: slow and damn slow."

A year ago, I willingly accepted primitive living conditions. Sometimes, though, my desires slow me down. My peace of mind and energies are sucked down the drain of impatience. I think I would be fine if I had a kitchen sink. And a bathroom. Jim gently points out, that if it isn't one thing, it'll be another.

Last month, I screamed and threw the old crusty pans down the hill rather than scrub them outside in cold water. Now this is the worst: small black slugs in my black cast iron pot.

I pile dirty pans, dishes and my mom's Mexican wine glasses into baskets in the doorway. After carefully climbing over them and down the tree stump steps, I carry the baskets across mud puddles, by way of tar paper stepping stones, out to the wash pan, which sits on the blue metal cart from the Wild Plum Café.

On foggy days when I can't see the forest or hear bird songs, ravens are a great help. Unseen in the mist, they fly overhead with powerful *whomping* wings. The pair reminds me that a larger world exists and my kitchen sink problems are relatively petty. Possibly two-thirds of the world's women wash dishes outside.

Although I complain, a favorite memory leaps into my mind's eye. After a dinner party for eight, all of my mother's fancy white plates, saucers and cups were lined up on the ground among bright green grasses. The parade of dishes remained planted there several days while rain prewashed them.

I could use paper plates, but I enjoy real dishes and choose not to waste more than necessary. Also, now that Jim has installed the water heater and rigged up a garden hose that reaches out to the dishpan, I do not mind the job.

One of the funniest childhood memories is of my eccentric father holding a tall stack of plates and saucers up high—claimed he was going to do a magic trick. Then he smashed them all on the floor. He did not want to wash dishes and he figured no one in the family should have to, either. My mom must have collaborated because she had purchased an enormous box of paper plates.When we ran out of paper plates, he tried to avoid cooking. We were fed a nutritious drink out of cans. Even he couldn't stand that, though, so we went back to cooking and washing dishes.

....So do I.

Water

Heater

On demand

Horizontal vent piping

Sheathing

Torpedo level pitch

Hot water valve

Shut off valve

Ball valve

Inlet

Union fitting

Sediment trap dirtleg

PEXcPvc adapter

Escutcheon

Discharge

Clean out

Tankless

Breaker swap

2-pole breaker

Neutral bus bar

Copper pipes

Elbows

Combustion air

Rubber flange

Pressure relief valve

Power cord

Coil

Pipe Dope

Snip and crimp

PEX tubing

Rancho Report: April 2005

Taking showers, washing dishes, laundry, dinner party

Our pianist friend, Rebecca, told us about the musical concept *tempo giusto*: sensitivity to pace and timing. Jim accepts the rhythm and work flow of the day. My life-long rush to check off To Do Lists, meet deadlines, scrutinize and fix problems has become a liability. I would like to enjoy life without fretting, without being grumpy about time wasted and projects undone.

I don't have mechanical talents or building skills, so I depend on Jim, who prioritizes daily tasks in an admirable way. He always makes time to notice nature. If he interrupts me while kneading bread or weeding or painting, I start to be annoyed. I go to him anyway and am surprised and exhilarated by his discoveries: the season's first shootingstar wildflowers, billowing 60 ft.-long spiderweb strands shimmering like rainbows. Bees on dandelions: each long stem bends from the weight of the bee so it looks like bungie jumping. I'm glad to help rescue a lizard with its head stuck inside a bay berry or remove a tick from our dog. We have enough time.

We invent ways to compensate for what we don't have. In lieu of a morning shower, I place fresh lavender on a fluffy, white face cloth in a round bowl patterned with blue flowers. Moistened with boiling water, the cloth quickly cools enough to drape over my face for a few luxurious, steamy moments. When removed, the cloth's evaporation is also refreshing. This ritual is as important as hot coffee.

We give each other showers on sunny days. On the knoll, we fill the watering can with cold water from the hose and stove-heated hot water. Jim sprinkles me, spring grass tickles my feet--I whoop and holler. On cold days, we sit before the fire and bathe using my mother's large hand-made bowl. Feet are scrubbed last. I am horrified, cannot believe they belong to me.

The outside throne overlooks a green glen polka dotted with buttercups. Contrary to my fears of discomfort in dismal, drizzly weather, I enjoy myself most of the time.

During dishwashing, I am entertained by woodpeckers working themselves up to a cacophanous crescendo. When they're not terrifying other birds with raucous squawks or raiding nests, ravens snort and softly *glock.* Stellar jays mimic the redtail hawk's cry, which begins on a high, shrill pitch and descends sharply. The saw-whet owl drives me nuts with too many monotone boop boops; I'm delighted when migrating song birds manage to get a word in edgewise. Washing dishes outside isn't horrible if you're not in a hurry and you have refreshing, bay-scented breezes.

The *casita's* front door opening is covered with tattered, stapled plastic. Tarpaper covers the exterior, windows do not yet exist, walls do not have insulation, flooring is raw plywood that's difficult to sweep. It is dark inside, but quilts hung on the walls take the sting off the cold. I am cheered because many of them are made by friends.

With temporary electrical wiring, Jim clipped a desk light onto the wall stud so that I'm able to paint. Instead of working on the yurt dining table, which must be cleared off for every meal, I enjoy my own space and work on my dad's large desk several hours each day. Making time to paint softens my frustrations with practical inconveniences. *Tempo giusto* kicks in.

Jim made several improvements that bring joy in my kitchen. He fit a plywood counter over my mom's bedroom set of chests so that slicing, dicing, and mixing is easy. Space for food preparation had been cramped. When I bumped the coffee pot with a full, wet filter, its brown liquid splashed and dribbled down the wall. While cleaning it up, I spilled a cup of beans, then knocked over a glass that crashed and shattered. I hit my crazy bone as I hoisted myself up.

Pantry shelves in the *casita* are lined with jars filled with every kind of dried legume and grain. Orange lentils

56

sit next to green split peas and red kidney beans. I make a variety of bread using six different kinds of flour. This morning's baking was awful: too much flax seed in pineapple bran muffins tasted like vitamin pills.

I am liberated from the one-a-half hour drive and two hour stint at the laundromat . To save time and money, instead of using driers, I used to return home with piles of damp laundry. Levis, sheets, shirts, underwear, socks were draped over boxes, ladders and the garden fence. Since Jim pulled the garden hose from the uphill spigot through the *casita* doorway, which is always open (because there's no door) into the washing machine, the laundry task is satisfying. I am amazed at modern technology and grateful to Jim for harnessing power from the sun and channeling water from the spring.

Recently, Merlín and Sito joined us for a dinner party with our niece, nephew and Jim's brother, Roger. We made flaming Greek cheese (fried thick slices of provolone with oregano doused with lemon juice.) We spread it on homemade French bread, followed by vegetable-venison stew, apples and chocolate chip cookies. Merlín played her *Jailhouse Rock* CD and we danced. She stood on Roger's shoulders, making elaborate flourishes like a circus star while we cheered.

Sometimes after school, Merlín makes "Early" Grey tea and Sito cooks *quesadillas*. He challenges Jim to a game of "Black"gammon. Their banter is lively as they bet marbles, quarters or M and M's. Merlín is learning to play Canasta. Having been an enthusiastic special education teacher for 24 years, I am overjoyed to play with these two.

Our two cats,The Wacko Brothers AKA The Joy Boys, are scampering and attacking each other in mid-air like wrestlers in the ring. They fight furiously, then retire to the side—eyes intent on each other, tails slapping the floor until one of them can't stand the tension and leaps to provoke another round. Eventually, they mosey over to the bed, falling asleep in each other's arms.

Both cats have soccer talent, especially when dribbling acorns. Grayman attacks leaves and sticks with great cunning. Unfortunately, the cats reach into cracks of dead logs for reptile prey and have earned the nickname Lizard Breath. We don't like to watch them gobbling down a rodent: *crunch, crunch* bones and all, only the little black tail left hanging out….and then nothing. Worst of all is finding two little ears and a tail with nothing inbetween.

Black Fang earned his latest nickname when his adult teeth grew in. When he sleeps on his back, all four legs are in the air, his head hangs off the bed, his yellow eyes at half-mast. His jaw opens slightly and the upper incisors, his fangs, expose a vampirish overbite.

We have enjoyed your calls and letters.

 Love,
Gretchen and Jim

MOUNTAIN LIONS AND WILD PIGS

Below the meadow we found a dead doe slit from gullet to zatch mountain lion style. Her bare rib cage caught my eye. We started to look closely, but quickly decided to not stand between the lion and its food. One day later, her carcass was dragged into the forest. After sitings like this, the news rapidly reaches all neighbors. We escorted Sito and Merlín to and from home. No one walked alone.

In the next valley, my friend encountered a mountain lion. She was in her outhouse when she heard a large creature casually strolling over dry leaves. She peeked through the screened window while the scruffy, dusty lion rested in the path. Thrilled with her good fortune, but frightened enough to be cautious, she waited and finally scared the wild cat away by slamming the door several times.

Most of us would love to see one of these magnificent animals. Ranchers appreciate the larger carnivores because they keep the deer population in check. They call deer "garden maggots." Neighbors also are glad the lions prey on wild pigs, which are overly abundant.

We had not been here long before I saw a black and white spotted pig, which was so enormous I thought it was a cow. Then I saw its short legs. Recently, we knew they were in our area because their bulldozer snouts had pushed up furrows of black soil throughout nearby meadows and slopes. As they search for grubs, bugs, roots, and acorns, their random ditches and pockets of upturned earth usually scar hillsides and cause erosion. My neighbor, though, notes that wild pigs also promote plant growth with their version of rototilling.

The night a pack of pigs surrounded the yurt two feet from our dream-laden heads, we didn't awaken because rain muffled their rooting and snorting. At dawn, a classic belch woke me up. I yelled, "PIGS!" and as I stuck my head out the door they disappeared down the back hill. As far as we could see, lumpy dark chocolate pudding landscaping replaced the grassy knoll and meadows. They mucked through the Wild Plum Café and near the spring, which was safely inside its fence. Our jaws opened in astonishment.

Neighbors tell us that since we have survived 108 inches of rain this season and a pig invasion, we are initiated. Folks put barbed wire at the bottom of fences, trap and shoot pigs, but must accept them as part of life. One neighbor had landscaped his clearing for a wedding. The morning of the celebration, he woke up to find devastation like ours.

GARDEN

Because of the pigs, we moved the garden fence to the top of the To Do List. We worked for a month pounding stakes and attaching deer, pig and rabbit wire fencing. To reach the top of each seven foot metal stake, Jim climbed to the top rung of a ladder perched on a steep slope. We levelled it with 2x4 shims and while Jim wielded the mallet, I kept him from toppling down hill by standing on the ladder's uphill side. On the top wire, I hung prayer flags made from brightly colored scraps from old clothes. May deer see the wire and not crash into it; may all go well on both sides. May everyone have enough to eat. The garden is more than 100 feet, so there's a lot of space for flags. And prayers.

Produce is not burgeoning, though. I'm highly motivated to learn ways to improve because the market is far away. Broccoli, beet and carrot seeds germinated, but don't seem to grow. Onions look like mere threads tentatively sticking up from black dirt. Carrot leaves have not yet feathered out. Lettuce is spindly. A local gardener assured me that when it warms up, plants will *streak!*

So far, only burr clover, bunch grass and other weeds thrive. Pulling up five wheelbarrow loads of weeds a day unleash a riot of smells: wild anise, parsley and arugula, moist dirt clods, musty mulch with plant friendly fungus mycelium.

While waiting for plants to become robust, I decorate the garden with stacks of tree trunk rounds, rocks and rusty metal junk salvaged from Palmer Canyon. Shovel and rake heads, engine parts and tools complement paths that meander in and around bean pole tipis, curved, square, or irregular plots.

Metal sculptures and paths winding around vegetables mixed with flowers satisfy the poet. Less visible is the network of tunnels dug by moles who eat insects around the clock. Their air pockets thwart the growth of seedlings. And what started out as an attractive mound of compost and straw for potatoes has become an earwig and sowbug palace.

On summer mornings, drops of water decorate the edges of squash, tomato and strawberry leaves. Jim says these sparkling necklaces are *gutation*, which is different from dew drops.

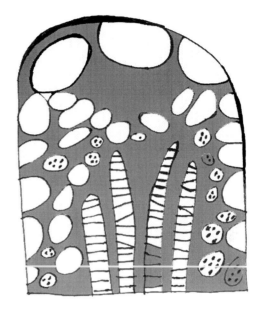

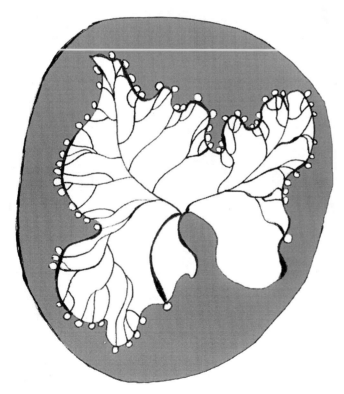

Plants have amazing ways to adjust internal moisture as temperatures and humidity change. At night, guard cells and stomata usually open to acquire or release water vapor.

However, when diffusion is difficult due to high humidity or soil that is too wet, the plant's Plan B kicks in. Root pressure squeezes moisture up the *xylem,* transporting it up the stalk, then into the network of leaf veins. At the end of the veins, the water vapor fills a chamber before it is released through slits along the leaf's edge. *Gutation* droplets are jewels.

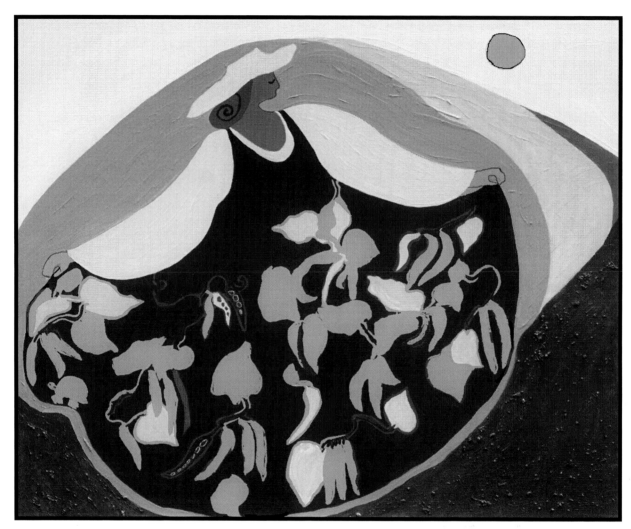

A friend gave me Romano bean seeds, which grow eight-feet high and provide food from July through October. Ten long pods make a meal for two. Their spectacular size and taste make them excellent gifts. When collecting seeds to save for the next season, I draw happy faces on the first robust pods from at least five plants. I don't pick those pods until they are mostly dry. They are shelled and saved in a cool, dry place all winter. In spring, I share these amazing seeds with other gardeners.

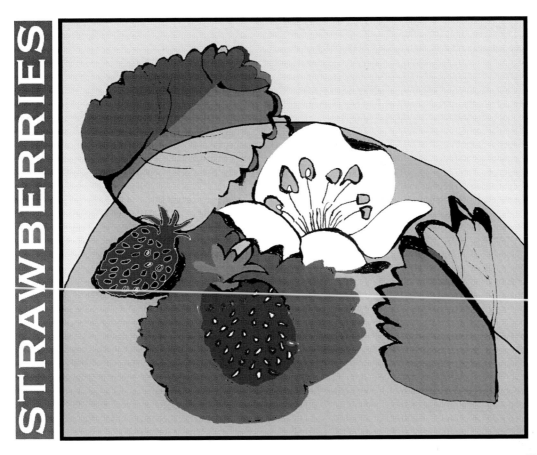

STRAWBERRIES

I longed for a strawberry patch like my mom's. Memories of sweet, succulent berries compelled me to make an enormous effort to nurture these plants. I have not taken the advice of a wise gardener who always had a prime garden because he didn't try to grow anything that didn't naturally thrive.

Strawberries have more predators than any other plant. Last summer, when natural grasses began drying, the doe severely pruned my small garden with the berries, edible flowers and herbs. I had heard that deer are repelled by the scent of ivory soap, so I tied dangling chunks of it from rudimentary wire cages over the berries. Since deer have a highly developed sense of smell, the garden book advised applying male cougar pee. Since that wasn't available, I squatted, peed and systematically claimed my ring of territory. She did not care. We and our dog slept nearby, and sometimes I awakened to find her munching or daintily picking her way through the Wild Plum Café on her way to or from strawberries.

She was stymied when we put up the eight-foot garden fence, but stellar jays moved in and plucked each berry moments before it was ripe. After securing bird netting over the patch of plants so that even I couldn't get in, beetles became the most thorough, systematic seekers of berry juice. They were somewhat thwarted after I tucked fine tulle net (the kind that ballet costumes are made of) around each cluster.

Since there was a plethora of these persistent bugs, I made beetle traps using a single berry for bait outside the netted area. The beetles have an attractive red outlining on black backs and are not scary to pick up. At first, I picked them up with gloves, but boldly abandoned squeamish feelings caused by desperate little legs in my hand. I visited the traps frequently, collected dozens of beetles and dropped them in a closed jar: the Doom Jar.

I don't enjoy combat with critters. I'm not like the guy who gleefully zaps colonies of earwigs with a torch. I carry eight-inch banana slugs on sticks far from the garden. Jim says that a sudden *lights out* approach is kinder than dropping insects into the Doom Jar for a slow death.

Predators were attracted to my weak plants. Since we had to conserve water, the strawberries were at risk because their roots were too dry. I became obsessed with mulch to help keep soil moist. Nearby, a mighty fir had fallen many years ago and had disintegrated to become its own shadow. Its decomposing bits of trunk and bark connected the entire branch structure in dramatic red-brown relief against black earth. Inside the stump, I accelerated the tree's return to earth with a garden claw, then scooped bark into the wheelbarrow.

I envisioned the dead tree living again in the form of abundant strawberries. Their dark green leaves were attractive next to the bark, but before long, I noticed there were only a few berries. I learned that bark and wood chips deplete nitrogen in soil.

After months of winter rain and a bag of steer manure, blossoms graced the garden. I cleared detritus, deported bugs and slugs, clipped strong runner vines between plants and held down the edges of netting with colorful broken dishes from last summer's wild plum kitchen car crash. Next week, we will enjoy homemade granola dazzled by strawberries.

RATTLER

Scarcely recognizable in dappled light under the oak, a large rattler stretches across the path. If I chase it with a stick and rocks, it will slither under the woodpile or house. In the heat of the day, it will stay cool under the porch, or at dusk it will soak up warmth on the gravel in the driveway.

Sooner or later our dog, who has already had a $1000 snake bite will provoke another. Or we'll step on it ourselves. These snakes often do not use their rattles for warning. I'm afraid of pigs and mountain lions, but I'm most afraid of rattlers.

A neighbor was bitten by one beneath her rabbit hutch and she almost lost her leg, almost died. That was ten years ago and her leg still hurts.

If Jim were home, he'd catch it with the snake stick, put it in a garbage can and drive it down to the creek. This snake stick is quirky, not in good shape for a novice like me. Even if I manage to slip the noose around the snake's head, it is far too heavy for me to lift into the garbage can. I'd drop it half way up.

I start to call the cats to chase it away, as they had last summer. As kittens, they had batted at a rattler as it reared up on its tail. Finally, it escaped their harassment and slid down the slope into the brush. This time, though, as they saunter up, I change my mind, fearing that they will be struck now that they're larger targets.

I consider what weapons are available and recall our neighbor's advice. Two days ago, Jesús complained that the hoe handle was too short for cutting a rattler.

I remember seeing a large rattler run over by a car on the main road.

Our car is conveniently positioned for the killing. Which I do.

I don't anticipate what an eon of time it takes for that long body to stop writhing. Its mighty body and tail rise, fall, gyrate. I scream, beg it to die, run over it two more times to shorten its agony. I'm horrified at what I've begun and cannot finish.

Our cat hunters approach, skitter sideways, swipe at the quivering tail rattles for an hour. Then they sit, vigilant.

Jim arrives and spies the gray and white patterned body before I am able to steer him away. He gently lectures me. All snakes are beautiful, helpful creatures. They eat rodents. They are a fact of life out here; this is their land, not ours. If you can't catch a rattler, chase it away with rocks.

He asks, "What are you going to do with it?"

I say I don't want to eat it the way he claims he would if he had a chance. I'll drive it to the top of the mountain, unless its fangs are embedded in my tire, causing me to have a violent flat and drive off the cliff to my own death. In the flat meadow above us, I'll stretch it out in the sunset so vultures can have it.

I want to honor its life, but how do I respect life while I am so afraid? I have good reason to fear and am sorry to have killed. Maybe a sunset mountain top ceremony would help.

"Let's walk it up to the top together," he says. "I'll carry it for you. I love you more than the snake."

"What will you carry it in?"

"In my hand!"

He drapes the great coil of gray snake in one hand. With the other, he holds my hand.

I feel a whisper of peace as we climb.

About half way up, he cxclaims, "I'm not going to carry this thing all the way to the top!"

He flings it over the hillside.

Not Much Sleep Lately

The snake episode has me rattled,
the garden drip line leaks,
voles and moles
undermine the pea patch.
I'm so tired I can scarcely
lift the paint brush,
so sleepy I don't finish
working on *Insomniac.*
I glance at the cats
hunkered over
a maimed sparrow,
manage to hoist my bulk
from the desk.
Unwilling feet in heavy boots
trudge to the trio.
The bird is not yet dead.
Mercifully, I smack the small head
sharply with a shovel,
then place it in the field,
beneath the vulture's passing shadow.

"AG" DAY

On "Ag" Day--the annual agricultural history event—I took art cards and prints to the small farmers' market on the ridge. The main event was the sheep round up. About 20 of us cheered the border collie as she herded ewes into the pen on the soccer field. At the same time, each spectator had a turn cuddling a newborn infant. In the background, two floppy-eared Nubian goats on leashes led children around the playground.

Women from the Kashia Reservation brought blackberry-huckleberry pies; the local lavender farmer brought home made oils and soaps; the elephant garlic farmer from Giant Mountain chatted with the jam and syrup woman from Precious Mountain. Greens, squashes, spring rolls, brownies and homemade fruit smoothies were delicious. There were as many vendors as customers, but that made the event even more charming.

The most exciting part of the day was Chicken Bingo. The kids collected 50-cent bets on which square of the plywood grid the chicken would poop on. My bet was square #20, but she did it on #23. The winning couple, from San Francisco, was on a honeymoon and happened to wander off the main road. They were thrilled to win $11.50.

Rancho Report: Sept. 2005

Water pump, the garden in my imagination

When our first year anniversary here arrived, I said to Jim, "Now we can read last year's journal and remember what we were doing."

"I know what I was doing," he said. "Panicking!"

As our local builder put it—if we had known what we know now, we might never have had the nerve to begin. This was the summer of the Big Fat Learning Curve. We're a micro-version of the blindfolded chess champions who play multiple games simultaneously. Except we make more mistakes and encounter more problems.

Recently, in the middle of our evening Canasta, Jim was going out on me for the sixth time when we heard a gunshot crack followed by a slow crash into brush. Another oak had fallen, which is why Jim constantly studies the health and structure of the oaks, bays and maples. The first part of each project tends to be felling a tree that is old or unhealthy and might fall on the structure. Our most important project this summer was to capture the spring water in a pipe, let it gravity feed to a holding tank and then pump it up to the main tank. But first we had to deal with the enormous dead maple that hung over the area. Two neighbors with four-foot long chain saws did the job.

After Jim built a small pump house and hooked up a complex network of pipes, he pounded stakes and fenced the entire area to protect it from wild pigs. Each of these accomplishments was difficult, but not as frustrating as when the pump would not work. One week he made six consecutive town trips for parts.

Each morning during the first half of August, Jim thought we'd have water by nightfall. Vegetables received minimum water, all our clothes were dirty. We wanted to avoid paying for another water delivery, but were so hot and dry we made an order for the next morning. Jim and Jesús put their heads together and finally got rid of air in the line. They immediately began pumping. I ran uphill to cancel the delivery one minute before the company closed.

With juice from solar panels, a network of electric lines and input/output/overflow pipes, valves galore, a ten- foot grounding rod pounded down to one inch, a small holding tank, and a finicky new pump we are enjoying delicious, clear water that has oozed from black mud under the bay tree.

We are able to splurge on watering the garden. I love to watch soil soak it up. Lettuce greens, basil, squashes, beans, onions, tomatoes, carrots and beets will become robust. Instead of searching under leaves for a dinner of zucchini, a few beans and undersized tomatoes, my basket will be overflowing with produce.

The dry season is almost over. Red brown bark peeling away from madrone trunks sounds like dripping water. Golden hillsides are burnished by morning and evening amber light. A lively, cool breeze from the north accompanies wild geese flying south. Summer insects have finished their cycle and rainy weather ticks have not yet begun theirs.

Thank you for keeping in touch.
Love, Gretchen and Jim

p.s. Merlín and Sito bring eggs with bright yellow yokes.

Dream

She is a cob of corn,
Husk peeling away, corn silk drying, falling,
Blowing to the west.
Kernels pop like sparks on a moonless night,
Leaving a bare cob that withers,
Disintegrates.
Her life force goes
Down the stalk, into the earth
Until she is ready to come up again.

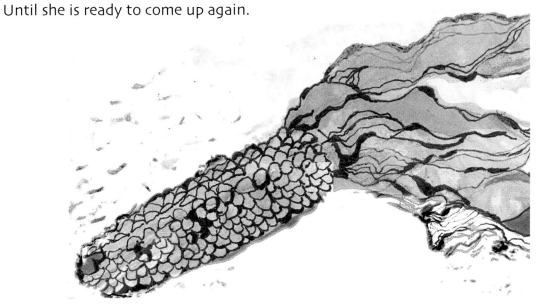

Underground:
last season's
composted squash and
bean vines,
egg shells,
coffee grounds
and filters,
oak and maple
leaves,
manure
from
Billy, our
neighbor's
horse.

Rancho Report: January 2006

Kick butt days, Hardie board, Darth Vader and Golum, kitchen sink

Fierce winds and sheets of rain are blasting the yurt all day. Jim's at the computer installing new virus protectors while Gray Man snuggles in his lap. Every time the walls and window coverings rattle and bang, the cat's pupils widen. When noise subsides, they become yellow slits again and he purrs.

We are not completely bonky on the fifth consecutive stormy day. We feel secure, fairly cozy and cheerful in this light-filled shelter. Never mind that it is so damp I must strike 28 kitchen matches to light newspaper, to light kindling, to light a morning fire.

One of the most generous things neighbors have done was to invite us to use their extra-long, pink bathtub on a rainy night. This first invitation from them was impromptu and included a delicious dinner of home-made sushi, spinach and mashed Hokaido winter squash from their garden. They have been here 18 years and keenly remember the early pioneer challenges. They lived for two years in a hand-crafted plastic greenhouse.

Before the first big rain, Jim and I put in kick butt days to finish waterproofing yurt doors, sills, lintels and circumference rim. Since we don't yet have a deck, Jim refastened the doors by standing on a milk crate on the 2x4 scaffolding supported by sawhorses. In order to reach the far upper corner to reattach wall coverings to major supports, he leaned out the open door, which is five feet off the ground. From the inside, I held his other leg so he wouldn't fall. We won't ever have to do that again.

The local contractor returned for the next phase of construction on the *casita:* double-paned windows, exterior siding and trim, gutters, rainspouts, and vents. Soffits protect the eaves so we won't need to scrape mildew when we're 80. The tattered plastic, stapled and restapled onto the doorway, is gone forever.

The *casita* exterior siding is rusty brown Hardie board planks, which are composite fiber-cement. If protected with paint or sealer, they are fire resistant and will last maybe forever. If left exposed to rain, they become cardboard, which disintegrates to mush and dust. I was highly motivated to touch up raw edges, nooks and crannies, especially around the precious on-demand flash water heater unit.

Merlín and Sito starred in the rainy day Canasta marathon. Merlín spoke like Golum in *Lord of the Rings,* while Sito maintained the character of Darth Vader throughout the game. They brought gift geodes, which we cracked open by whacking them with a hammer. The kids told us that the lumpy, gray balls were formed in cavities of sedimentary rock. After they hardened, groundwater carrying minerals seeped into the hollow spaces. Our geode interiors contain quartz designs in milky white and gray.

The most important news: we enjoy an indoor kitchen sink. The $10 cast iron double sink from the county's Recycle Town sat in tall grass for a year and a half because we had no idea how long it takes to move down the To Do list. Jim made a pywood counter top with a round backsplash that fits the yurt. I painted it bright blue with phases of the moon.

My sweetie wants me to include this: he was pummeled willy-nilly by shifting winds of uncertainty caught in the grip of mysterious forces and now leads a simple, Spartan life enslaved to the mission of making me comfortable.

Love,
Gretchen and Jim

ASPARAGUS

Last year, I avoided digging as I prepared for planting. I am not a buff sort of gal. A friend gave me instructions for a *lasagna* garden, which sounded delicious and claimed to be easy. Instead of weeding and digging, I put down layers of newspaper and dozens of wheelbarrow loads of mulch from under the bay tree. Wood chips and fireplace ashes were also layered.

By March, I was smug, more than ready for what I thought would be a lush, thriving garden. Each bed for future beets, broccoli, lettuce, onions, squash and beans had been layered and decorated with towers of rusty junk and rock stackings. By summer, though, I discovered I had cultivated the tiniest mini-crops in existence: beets the size of cherries, squash like baseballs,

79

sparse, ragged heads of broccoli on bent, spindly stalks.

I resolved to work up the energy to dig. Since aparagus needs to develop a root system in a trench two feet deep, I learned to wield a pick ax. Jim taught me to swing it overhead, make eye contact with the spot to be "plowed," put a few springs back into my knees as I heave the ax forward, let gravity grab the heavy iron as it falls to earth. This has become my new sport. I like the way my upper arms and lower back feel. After ten swings I'm warm, breathing hard, and have the satisfaction of never missing my target.

When I started digging the trench, Merlín and Sito wanted to try the ax. They made up the five-swing rule. When my turn came, they exclaimed, "You're good!" Since I've never been good at sports, I glowed. The asparagus trench excavation reconfigured my identity, gave me confidence and prompted me to improve all veggie beds with better soil preparation.

As the asparagus grew, I gradually filled the bed with mulch and dirt. Their delicate, feathery leaves billowed out and provided shade for a lounge chair in summer. In the fall, after turning yellow orange, the brittle stalks were cut close to the ground. I shoveled mulch and manure over the bed so that heavy rains would soak the roots with nutrients.

This year, asparagus is the first vegetable to poke through winter ground. Fifteen slender stalks boldly emerge and shoot up an astonishing six or eight inches in a day. When other plants are bent by harsh rains, asparagus stands straight up. The root system needs to continue developing, though, so I harvest only half the crop the first season.

We are surprised that fresh asparagus is tastier and sweeter than that from the store. Grilled, broiled, boiled, in a soup or raw: we cannot eat enough.

CLOTHES

On a blustery April morning, Jim started laughing and called me "Mrs. Potato." I was bundled up and puffed out with my usual plaid work shirt buttoned over a bulky sweater and thick vest.

My disregard for appearances--especially clothes--contrasts with my attention to carefully chosen outfits in the past. Throughout my 23 years of teaching, one of the ways I surprised my students was to wear new combinations of shirts, skirts, pants, vests. They often noticed every detail and reinforced my penchant for interesting fabrics and accessories.

Once, my second grade reading group must have been overdue for some fun because they all but fell off their chairs laughing when they noticed my Christmas socks--it was April.

I felt so strongly about the importance of clothes as an extension of a person's identity that I was one of the most vociferous opponents of school uniforms. For twenty years, children on our playground were like a garden of colorful flowers. The parents finally forced a change in policy so that freedom of expression through clothes was not valued as highly as constraints, controls and safeguards for youngsters.

In those days of juggling the roles of mother, teacher and artist, I escaped by seeking treasures on thrift store bargain racks or swapping clothes with friends. We piled a mountain of used clothes (many of them only slightly used) on the livingroom rug and critiqued each other's new fashion statements. I especially liked recycled clothing (such as the sea mist silk shirt and brown velveteen jacket) because they were previously enjoyed by friends.

My favorite clothes memory: I was in jail along with 28 other women arrested for trespassing at the Nevada Test Site in the mid-1980's. On the first of seven nights, we were in the Tonopah jail holding cell with no beds. We huddled on a cold cement floor with a few sheets. Our clothes and belongings had been recorded, bagged, locked away. We were strangers, and although we wore identical navy blue jumpsuits, we decided to entertain ourselves with a fashion show.

After experimenting with what we had, we presented ourselves, one by one. Used white paper coffee cups, strung together with shoelaces, became earmuffs or hats or bizarre bras worn on top of the dark suits. Other paper cups became armature for bustles beneath sheets. Cups with the bottom end facing out became binocularesque eye pieces. We fashioned togas, veils, swirling dance skirts with sheets and jumpsuits inside out or upside down. *Too ridiculous* was not in our vocabulary. Each one of us was spectacular and lovely.

My attitudes about clothes began to shift during the twenty minute wildfire evacuation. As I left our bedroom closet, I was aware of brushing against the unique black suede jacket, the intricately appliquéd Hmong dress, the Peruvian and Guatemalan weavings and other hand-made favorites for the last time. One of dozens of split-second decisions was to leave all my clothes.

The morning after, friends and strangers delivered clothes, which I was delighted to share with the other women from our burned canyon community. At the end of the first meeting, I tied scarves to the top of our station wagon's open tailgate. The filmy, colorful fabrics waved in the breeze and attracted attention to displayed business suits, socks, shoes and every type of casual wear. Generous donors had provided variety and quantity so that each woman found something genuinely pleasing, perhaps helping her to remember who she really was.

Most days here in our new life, there's not a soul in sight other than Jim. I am lucky because he sees beauty everywhere: shimmering spider web strands, designs of landscape, backlit weeds, shadow and texture of tree bark, the wave in my hair. He often has a Buddha twinkle in his eye that comes with accepting what is. Instead of dismissing his point of view as crackpot because it is way too uncritical, I have learned to let it bathe me in tranquility.

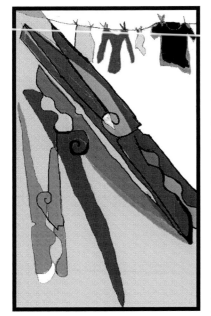

We each have a town outfit, clean and without tatters, but since most days are spent working on the land, we often wear the same outer uniform for over a week. As months and years pass, we become sick of seeing the same clothes on each other. Tension mounts as the time for the rip off-each-other's-clothes ceremony approaches. We each choose one garment belonging to the other and we gleefully destroy it in a winter bonfire. We don't reveal the targeted black-listed clothing item until the appointed hour. I don't know if I will be relieved or sorry.

On Washing Day, the sunny one between many rainy ones, I drop what I'm doing and load my solar powered washing machine. Pinned to the top fence wire, clothes billow and flap in a row of deliberately arranged colors and shapes. One of our neighbors hangs her clothes out according to the color wheel sequence. We aging women, in aprons and floppy sunhats, get a kick out of performing daily tasks by waking up to all our senses.

I enjoy watching clothes wear out. Acquisition in reverse: thrift store levis and shirts be come frayed and faded until they"graduate" to the rag bag. Jim celebrates his worn out work shirts by spontaneously ripping them off, making the buttons fly in grand *Hulk* style.

We are not the only ones who wear levis with permanently dirty knees or hastily repaired jackets. One friend puts patches on with Hard as Nails construction glue. Folks wear duct tape on vest rips and pant leg holes are earned, not paid for because of a brand name.

On special occasions, though, ranch folks dress up. At a recent party, in lieu of gifts, the birthday man requested that the women wear skirts. There was a Hawaiian print sundress, a long, sleek silk skirt with a slit up to the thigh, a filmy, swishy nylon skirt and several calico gathered skirts.

My favorite community event is Halloween. Among the grown-ups dressed as vampires, dragons, green chickens, giant pumpkins, bandits (with real bullets in the bandolier) is the young, usually scruffy, backhoe operator. He disguises himself with a clean shave, slicked back hair and the scariest costume he could think of: a three-piece suit.

At our local farmer's market, we wear the less-faded hats, colorful scarves and dangling earrings. The urge to be decorated cannot be denied. We live within a tribe and like to be noticed. We each make a contribution to the group, but we are also enjoy looking at each other. We wear something that adds zest.

When I reorganized our cargo container storage area, I realized that for someone committed to living a simple life with a fresh chance to live unencumbered with stuff, I had accumulated too many clothes. They were functional, but drab. I wanted to go shopping and choose a new dress to replace the donated one.

When I started to write this, I thought I had lost interest in clothes. I discover that I see much of life in terms of a many layered and continually changing wardrobe. I notice what people wear, my current paintings have women with fabulous outfits. The landscape outside my window seems to be fabric over the hills. Dun-colored fringes from last August's wild oats accent April's bright green grass, which will become dresses and cloaks covering hills and vales in May. Trunks and limbs that are dark brown with tightly curled moss in summer, are now wearing chartreuse chenille sweaters.

Rancho Report: May, 2006

Woodpeckers, frost, fava beans, cow invasion, cats

This morning, our first breakfast coffee steamed up as sun streamed through open doors. Pileated wood-peckers drummed in a stereophonic jam session. They sound like jackhammers or make rapid, low drum beats from trees with large, deep hollows and high tones from pecking on smaller trunks and snags.They're doing major construction projects for spring nests in the firs and oaks, which have buds on every twiglet.

In February, Jackie Frost's gift of sunlit diamond rained down from gnarled, mossy oak limbs. Jim gently knocked frozen water out of garden dishes and threw the transparent discs like Frisbees so they crashed into sparkling shards. The little citrus trees looked like ghosts with their nightly sheet coverings, but all survived.

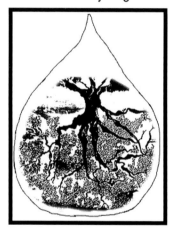

During spring showers, we stared through the rain-spattered French door windows. Jim discovered that by looking through a single raindrop, he could see an entire upside down oak. We also learned more about the unseen: oaks have long roots and often join each other underground.

May's warmth prompts blooming: electric blue Dutch iris contrast with California poppies. Daffodils, red, yellow and pink tulips have come and gone. Chard stalks are shocking magenta, gold and bright green. Blue batchelor buttons, seven-foot high foxgloves and Oriental poppies attract bees. The most robust crop is fava beans, which we eat in every imaginable form: in omelettes and salads, soups and casseroles; they are boiled, stir-fried or mashed into a bright green dip, which we scoop up on contorted, slug-pocked carrots. The Wild Plum Café is open every day.

Our animal adventure this month features cows. At dawn, I hear heavy breathing on the other side of the thin wall covering. Two enormous black cows are rubbing and leaning on the yurt. They and their two young ones have escaped their fenced pasture to forage on oak leaves and spring greens. Their tongues sweep and slurp a 12 inch diameter of grass as they take their sweet time circling the yurt. They're doing a good job of saving Jim from weed whacking and I wouldn't mind, except that large cow pies planted on our doorstep are not fun to clean up.

Jim, in his yellow slicker, goes out in the rain with a flimsy yardstick to herd them away. He commands them with "Shoo, git along there, doggies!" Both half-ton black angus placidly stare at him and continue munching.

These cows have been roaming the hillsides for two months, but they're often in ravines and gullies, hidden glens and forests, so it is hard to catch them. That morning, though, when we call Cowboy Bob, he comes down immediately. He is confident, doesn't need to yell or threaten as he calmly walks behind the lumbering creatures and guides them home.

This evening, Gray Man is sprawled out before the fire, taking half-hearted swipes at the twitching black tail belonging to Stretch, who is draped over the chair above him. (We used to call the black cat Black Fang, but now he's lank and measures 36 inches from nose to tail tip.) He finally notices the annoying sensations. In a flash, he intends to attack his brother, but ends up biting his own tail.

Love,
Gretchen and Jim

p.s. "Pileated" comes from pileum, the crest of head feathers.

87

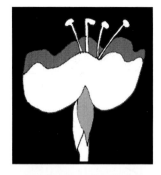

Wild Flowers

Andrew's Clintonia
California poppy
Hendersen's shooting star
Miner's leaf
Wild onion
Hillside gooseberry
Fritillary
Red Ribbons
Western columbine
California wild rose
Pacific rhododendron
Canyon delphinium
Wild azalea
Pennyroyal
Sticky monkey
Pacific madrone
Farewell to spring
Douglas iris
Coast mule ears
Soap plant
Wild hyacinth
Popcorn flower
Forget-me-not
Common yarrow
Woodland strawberry
Baby blue eyes
California buttercup
Ithuriel's spear
Lupine
Golden Fairy Lantern

The first purchase for our new home was an extra-long cast iron bathtub. As I decorated it, I imagined we would soak in a steamy winter bath house the first rainy season. That was two years ago.

This spring, we had planned to work on the bathroom, but it rained so much we did not have a single dry day to go to town for sheet rock. When planning the two *casita* rooms, we measured the bathroom so exactly that the room had to be built around the tub. It is so large that there isn't room to install the toilet before the tub. Since the tub has no legs, Jim has to make a cradle from hefty 6x6 beams. Before he accomplishes this task, he must crawl underneath the flooring and do plumbing. He says every job depends on another job.

It's not easy to build a bathroom and it has been demoted to the bottom of the To Do List. Jim's reasoning: during pleasant weather, we don't *need* an indoor bathroom. Sitting on the throne overlooking the glen is an exquisite experience.

The current hot water shower routine is much better than last year's. We take turns standing on the edge of the yurt door and squirt hot water from the garden hose on each other. He doesn't mind.

CREEK DAYS

Spring picnics at the creek includes picking wildflowers. Merlín and Sito decorate Jim's beard with small blue Bird's-Eye Gilia and Blue Dick. Merlín, with her blue skirt backlit by sunshine, looks like a flower herself. As we loll on mossy banks under dappled greenery, the kids cross the stream on a fallen oak branch bridge. They make increasingly daring leaps across freezing cold water. Standing on the culvert ledge, we float wood pieces downstream and drop large sticks in swirling eddies.

On the uphill walk home, our third grade warrior rolls the largest boulders possible over the embankment. We cheer if they make it to creek bottom. When he discovers skinks under rocks, he dangles one by the tail in his sister's face. When she stomps off, he teases her, then returns the creature to its home.

90

Wild Plum Café  Calendar

January: New leaves.
February: White blossoms buzz with bees.
March: Petals flutter like confetti.
April: Green plums the size of bb's.
May: Plums the size of peas.
June: Plums like cherries, tart, juicy,
                plucked from the tree, plumb and firm,
                sticky, squishy, red-purple ones
                for boiling jams, juice, syrups to spread
                and drizzle on pancakes and pandowdies,
                for baking pies, oatmeal crisps and cobblers,
                for the Wild Plum Café with squawking jays,
                acorn woodpeckers and bossy ravens
                making a ruckus as they join the party.
July: Black, dry plums and pits.
August: Yellow leaves.
September: Orange leaves.
October: Brown leaf litter carpet.
November: Bare branches.
December: Bud swellings.

SHOOTING STARS

Jim installed a neighbor's cast-off cast iron tub in the Summer "Bath House." As dainty white soap plant flowers open, stars begin shining. We soak in hot water, chat quietly. Leisurely discussions meander from the morning's dewy spider webs that look like snowflakes in the meadow's gold grass stubble to the next strategy for keeping the doe out of the garden. We ponder the gopher snake poking his head out of the mole hole, how soon the plums will ripen, where to plant five kinds of berries so that we can eat them from May to November.

We're spellbound by the Milky Way on ordinary nights. One night, though, I scream and point to a fireball streaking from the moon. The head glows yellow with a chartreuse halo while the tail flames are bright orange across half the sky. The spectacle lasts long enough for Jim to turn around from his end of the tub before it winks out behind the oaks on the horizon.

Wikipedia reports that millions of meteors enter earth's atmosphere every day. They ram into the outer part of the mesosphere, which is 53 miles up and -130 degrees Farenheit, with such force that they glow and burn. Melted particles and gas become trails of light. Only a few meteors blast through the mesosphere and become "earth-grazing fireballs." The yellow and chartreuse halo around our ball of fire is probably caused by iron and copper particles.

We've rocked and rolled to Jerry Lee Lewis's , but never expected to see one. Every August, Perseid meteors shower, blip on and flicker out one per minute. Some burst into view with strong white light becoming blue as they fade, some jump out of the Big Dipper like popcorn. That is extraordinary, but this wild streak of fire takes my breath away. My heart skips.

My fascination for starry skies began decades ago during visits to the High Sierras. In Southern California, city lights pollute night skies so that people have limited experience with stars. After the 1994 Northridge earthquake knocked out power lines in Southern California, there were many calls to newspapers and police because folks were alarmed by the bright glow in the heavens, which they had never seen before. I was lucky, though, to have had summer nights in the high mountains, where cold, crisp air jerked me awake while shooting stars dazzled me speechless.

During a period when I was heartbroken, I drove nine hours to visit a friend at Echo Lake. One night watching starry skies refreshed me before I had to drive back to L.A. to begin the school year. On that long trip—crying the entire way--I realized that stars are there all the time. Although invisible, they can be a source of spiritual energy whenever I need them.

Note Left for House Guest

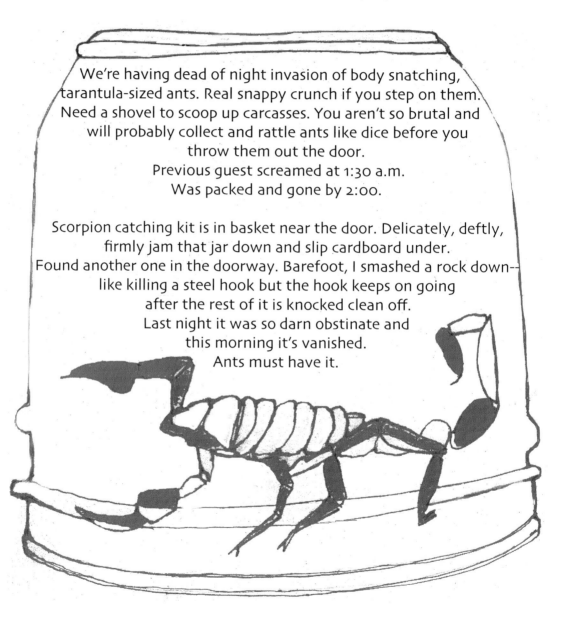

We're having dead of night invasion of body snatching,
tarantula-sized ants. Real snappy crunch if you step on them.
Need a shovel to scoop up carcasses. You aren't so brutal and
will probably collect and rattle ants like dice before you
throw them out the door.
Previous guest screamed at 1:30 a.m.
Was packed and gone by 2:00.

Scorpion catching kit is in basket near the door. Delicately, deftly,
firmly jam that jar down and slip cardboard under.
Found another one in the doorway. Barefoot, I smashed a rock down--
like killing a steel hook but the hook keeps on going
after the rest of it is knocked clean off.
Last night it was so darn obstinate and
this morning it's vanished.
Ants must have it.

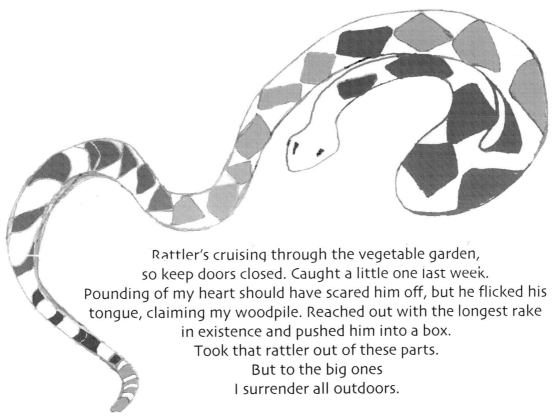

Rattler's cruising through the vegetable garden,
so keep doors closed. Caught a little one last week.
Pounding of my heart should have scared him off, but he flicked his
tongue, claiming my woodpile. Reached out with the longest rake
in existence and pushed him into a box.
Took that rattler out of these parts.
But to the big ones
I surrender all outdoors.

Step mindfully day and night,
(night is inky black under canyon oaks)
when quadraphonic crickets blot out everything in your
mind--except
the scream of the mountain lion.

Bring that plump, juicy dog inside
before you go to sleep.

95

WOOD SHED

The woodshed has a dirt floor, tin roof, and is decorated with rusty masks salvaged from Palmer Canyon. Jim mocks the world of high tech crime detection with his defunct binocular surveillance system. With dry wood stacked to the rafters of the new shed, our home fires burn more readily. Maple, bay, and oak have been drying for a year; two cords are split, kindling is ready.

Jim's new log splitter cuts through hefty rounds of oak as if they were butter. We split, load and stack 50 times more wood per hour than before. Jim sits on a stump while holding a large chunk under the blade. He collects a jumbled mountain of branches and trunks on one side, then

96

throws the split chunks on the other. He reminds me of the girl who spun straw into gold in Rumplestiltskin. However, he isn't thinking of stories. He focuses on avoiding scorpions as he picks up each chunk of wood before carefully placing it under the blade.

We become warm even before we light the fire in the stove. Each piece is handled ten times: hoist the chain-sawed trunk round into the truck bed, throw it into the wood pile, place it onto the wood splitter's orange plate under the hydraulic-activated wedge, toss the chunk into the split pile, lift it into the wheelbarrow, stack it in the shed. After the wood has dried for six months and when cold weather arrives, we place split logs from the woodshed back into the wheelbarrow, guide it to the yurt and fill the indoor wood holder, then transfer it into the stove. The final move: carry ashes to the garden.

Until now, we've kept piles of wood under green, blue and brown tarps that become rodent and scorpion hotels and eventually leak. We'd get wet as we lifted the tarp. Pockets and pools of rainwater slid down the inside of our sleeves as we searched for the best of the perpetually damp logs. Fires were smoky and hard to start.

Sometimes Jim moved a pallet of wood without lifting a single piece. I thought he was crazy the first time he announced his plan. I helped him *walk the dog* by placing pcv pipe rollers under the full pallet while he leveraged it up with a long bar resting on a fulcrum. Inch by inch the pallet moved. I was impressed.

At night, in lieu of television, we watch the fire through the stove's glass door. Small flames lick around kindling and medium chunks. Moss, bright green, soft and spongy last season, is stiff and dry on the log's bark. It catches quickly, its red curls glow as three or four logs slowly become a roaring blaze. Knot holes resemble winking monster eyes and pulsing embers make it easy to imagine adventurers lost within caves surrounded by volcanoes.

A friend asked if building the comforting wood stove fire every night reminds us of the devastation wrought by the '03 wild fire. The question prompts a memory. Watching flames leap a hundred feet high, an inferno spanning miles of a Prussian blue horizon, we forgot ourselves before staggering, awesome beauty.

97

Red and Yellow Dinner

Yellow tablecloth with crimson poppies
Velvety scarlet dahlias with yellow pistils
Bees wax candles with a warm glow
Ruby red plates
Yellow-orange napkins with lemon designs

Appetizers: fried yellow squash blossoms, Jujube cherry tomatoes, gorgonzola cheese on fried zucchini round slices garnished with yellow pansies, tomato chutney on crackers

Red zinfandel from the local vintner

Pizza: red sauce from Principe Borghese tomatoes, Golden Marconi peppers, Serrano red peppers, Yellow Boy tomatoes, cheddar cheese

Two-tone soup: pureéd seasoned red peppers and tomatoes; pureé seasoned summer squash with onion. Place a small empty can with both ends cut out in a bowl. Pour the red soup on the outside of the can, then pour the yellow soup in the inside. Remove the can, garnish with calendula petals

Yellow cake with red geranium petals on top

Red Bush tea

Whole Wheat Loaf:

1 T active yeast in warm water
1 summer night
3 C hot water
1 C nuts
1/2 C honey
1 rising moon

1 C equal parts: curiosity, wheat germ
5 C flour
1/2 C olive oil
10,000 dancing stars
Bake: 350 degrees Wait: that long
Makes: enough

FRENCH CAFÉ

MENU MENU

SON

POP'S

MENU

DINCKERS

RADER BLADER

TINE VINE

ZON ZAY
(COMES WITH ANY AP.

SQUISH

ZELINDA'S

CUYA

RED FLAPPERS

JACQUE ZOOZAM FLAN

WALKER TALKER

ZATER

TIFFEE

A.P.P.

TROPICAL JANGLE

POPPER POPPES

ZIZZARTS

CAPTAIN ROOKIE

ZANGO FREAK

ZINKLES

PELLOW PILLS

SIMMON PER S

ZUCKERRS

C.B.P.

Merlín and Sito recently saw *The Pink Panther,* which highlights Steve Martin's terrible French accent. The kids were in the mood to create a French Café dinner for their parents. They planned and cooked most of the meal: cookies, teriyaki chicken, baked squash, salad from the garden, and a dozen other small, un-French items such as hot sauce and chocolate balls wrapped with foil to look like eyeballs. They renamed each dish, wrote the entire menu in fake French so that no one knew what they were ordering. Merlín placed labels on the food arranged on the kitchen counter so that she would be able to translate the orders. Flowers, candles, and Edith Piaf's French music enhanced the ambiance. Sito greeted his parents with a towel over his arm and guided them to the table. At first, we conversed carefully with almost intelligible semi-English words. As the meal progressed, we chattered with heavy, fake French accents and exaggerated Italian gestures.

100

RAVEN JAMBOREE

The day before our raven pair hosted a party for their clan, they made raucous caws back and forth from seven locations throughout the valley. Never having heard a network of communication like this, we were surprised at the size of the local raven community.

Early the next morning, scores of shiny blue-black birds glided, circled, twirled above and around the large bay tree near the spring. With loud flapping wings, small groups descended and joined the fest. The *kaaa, aarck!* cacophanous din increased with each arrival.

101

The event seemed to have been planned for flocks from the north. Since these birds live about 15 years, perhaps they were excited to be reunited with old buddies and children. They partied most of the day. Varying tones and intensities ranged from harsh to soft cawing and *prruk, crruck aarck* croaking.

That evening, the raven guests flew off to roost. The next morning, there was further communication between the valley's raven homes. This time their vocalizations were almost entirely soft *glocking* and metallic *tok tok tok*.

Later, a fly-by of hundreds caught my attention. They were so high I could scarcely hear the occasional *"kaaa."* I wondered where their next stop would be.

Rancho Report: November '06

Petrichor, ticks, phantom ticks, bath tub, first flush, music

We welcome winter rain and eagerly anticipate the first shower's fragrance, which is called petrichor. During the dry season, dust and dirt absorb oils from plants and trees. According to *Wikipedia,* Greeks named this rain *Ichor* (the fluid from the veins of the gods) because it releases a scent as it mingles with *petro (*stone or earth.*)* Inhaling spicy essences of bays, oaks, dried flowers and grasses, we become intoxicated.

During the rainy season, earth and forest duff cushion my footsteps, making it easier to hike on deer trails and scramble up ravines. Trees awaken, unfurling spongy, feathery soft, deep green moss. I hug them.

While driving on the hard-packed dirt roads, we enjoy washed, shiny vehicles. This contrasts with summer's red road dust, which blankets our car so heavily that the gas station attendant exclaims, "You could grow a garden on your car! I'm going to save your life, I'm going to wash your windows, no, I'm going to wash your car!."

The only upsetting detail about the rainy season is ticks. They flourish in damp weather. Black legged deer tick larva and nymphs attach themselves onto small mammals. After sucking blood, they drop to the ground and molt several times. As adults, they climb blades of grass, stretch out their front legs and wait for us to brush against them. We constantly check our dog for bloated ticks. If we don't drop these mini-monsters into the Doom Jar, the females could crawl into cracks and lay about 2,000 eggs.

Ticks transmit more diseases world wide than any other arthropod. Around here, we are on alert for the bull's eye red ring, an indication of Lyme's Disease, which has a variety of symptoms. A bite without disease pathogens is bad enough. My bites become swollen, red, itchy welts for ten days. The sooner we pull out the tick head, the better. Once their saliva hardens like cement and the tick engorges, it is difficult to yank it out. We carry tick tweezers, but our neighbor pries them out with his pocket knife, then gleefully slices them on his pant leg.

We also have a neuro-psychological reaction. For every tick bite, a hundred phantoms attack. I feel a tickle, a pinch, an itch, a pin prick pain and yell for Jim to come and inspect me. He finds nothing.

Bath tub progress: Jim plumbed, insulated and dry-walled the bathroom. He prepared the brick platform and redwood cradle for the 300-pound tub. Jesús zoomed down on his 4-wheeler before going to work so he could help lift it into place. We moved and nestled it by using the car jack and pvc pipe rollers. Now that the tub's out of the way, the toilet will be bolted down. We might make the first flush tonight.

Huddling over a seven-inch screen before the fire, we had enjoyed watching movies. However, our small laptop heated up and shut off so often during the plot's climax, we gave it up. Instead, we play music. Jim has been playing with a traditional West African drum group. He packs his two-foot *dundunba,* the smaller *sang ban*, their stands, sticks and bells, then drives two hours each way every Thursday night. While driving, he taps out rhythms on the steering wheel. He comes home feeling elated.

For my birthday, Jim had an electric piano delivered. My fingers are coming alive again on this seven-octave keyboard, which behaves and sounds like a real piano. I am so crazy for ragtime that I'm going to learn every Scott Joplin piece before I die.

Thank you for keeping in touch. If you email us, please do not send photos. Our phone line connection becomes seriously constipated when faced with large messages. Our inboxes were tied up for two weeks by photos. Jim drove two hours to town to use a high-speed internet connection in order to download and sift through 200 inbox items.

Yours,
Gretchen and Jim

STRANGER

On my way back from town at dusk, I rounded the bend to find a young man resting on his duffel bag. This was a long and lonely stretch with no houses, no abandoned shelter, no people, hardly ever any cars and it was starting to rain. I inspected him carefully during a conversation through the window and concluded he was benign.

He was on his way to the Buddhist retreat, which was more than 20 miles away. He was clear-eyed, lean, fit and in his 30's--about the same age as my own kids. His long hair was wet and straggly. (Later, you could see each ringlet outlined in gold.) Although exhausted, he had a peaceful presence. I invited him for dinner, lodging, and a ride to the monastery the next day.

105

I have refused hitchhikers for decades. But in this case, I had a light feeling in my body. When I was young and traveling the world, people took me in. Greek villagers, Italian country families, German, Danish, Norwegian and French strangers befriended me and enriched my outlook on the world. What a different and refreshing time that was; now I could give back, help create a tidbit of the trust we had in earlier times.

I've known a few young men like Bracken. They are on a spiritual journey, guided mostly by intuition. Maybe they are *bodhisattvas* who spread light and give practial asistance to those of us struggling along. They walk lightly on the earth and have a twinkle in their eye as if they might know something we don't. They enjoy being jesters and fools.

Bracken described his life history during the half hour drive. He had started back east, biking with a cart, which carried a cello and gear to the Rainbow Festival in Wyoming. With a hat ready to receive coins, he and Agnes (his cello) performed to earn money for food. Jack of many trades, Bracken did odd jobs wherever possible as he wandered west. In the last town, his cart broke, so he sold it along with the bike. Having read about the retreat center in the hills to the west, he headed out on foot.

At a bend in the road, I interrupted Bracken so that he would pay attention and look at the changing landscape. He claimed he was watching--multi-tasking. One moment later, we were awestruck. He asked, "What kind of a witchy woman are you?" because on the side of the road was a golden eagle. These birds are rare and here before us was an incredible specimen eating a skunk. We were so close we could see the pupils in his eyes as he studied us. Each golden feather was outlined in a slightly darker shade.

Jim and I usually consult each other on all plans, but since this wasn't possible, I had qualms about how he might react to taking in a stranger. It was dark and rainy when we burst through the door. Jim was taken aback, even alarmed, but he was gracious. While I prepared dinner, our guest warmed himself by the wood stove, introduced Agnes, closed his eyes and settled into a mellow medley ranging from Bach to lively gypsy tunes. Jim joined in with drumming. I was grateful for musical bridges to close the gap filled with questions and anxiety.

106

During dinner, Bracken continued to lay out his life story: two young daughters, work as a masseur, short-order cook, waiter in a coffee shop where his boss wanted her employees to be fully present and serve "radiant" coffee to customers. That was where he learned that some people just want a cup of coffee.

In the morning, after a breakfast of hearty nine-grain cereal with plump golden raisins, Jim took me aside. "What if the monks don't take him? This guy would like to camp here and…"

"Oh, he'll figure it out," I said airily. "Buddhist monks will be compassionate and won't drive a weary, good-hearted man into a rainstorm. Besides, he's made his way this far, hasn't he? Something will open up."

I'm often jealous of my time, don't like to break my workflow to drive around the countryside. However, to be sure our traveler was well on his way, I drove him 45 minutes to the monastery. I dropped him and Agnes off, drove home through rain squalls satisfied that I had done the right thing.

Late that afternoon, a neighbor called. He had just passed a stranger, a dark figure trudging up their road. He had an enormously tall backpack with something that could be a weapon of unknown destructive force. He was looking for Jim and Gretchen, so the neighbor explained how to backtrack to the missed turn.

Our neighbor said, "Being a good Samaritan is fine, but you never know. These are difficult times for the unemployed, homeless, ragged, dragged down, drugged up and zoned out. We are uneasy and don't like strangers wandering around on our land."

Jim's worst fears bloomed. The fellow that we didn't know could be hard to get rid of. We treasure our solitude. A confrontation loomed. We dread confrontations. M heart thudded at the thought of it. As another neighbor once said, "No good deed goes unpunished."

I was about to go looking for the Bracken in the dark when he showed up, drenched and anxious. He explained that the monks were chanting all day every day this week. They wouldn't make spur-of-the-moment decisions about anyone on their doorstep no matter how wet the weather or how cold the season.

I'm sure they had a satisfied feeling when they gave him a packet of snacks and drove him 45 minutes to where the main paved road met our dirt one.

Bracken was sopping wet. We were gracious. I steered him to a hot bath to warm him up. This was a small gesture compared to the sacrifices many folks make to help others. But what was this heavy feeling in my body? Our guest was clean, neat, polite, reasonably helpful, had a wonderful vocablary, quoted Rumi with ease, had those golden ringlets. But his propensity to talk too much drove me nuts. We are accustomed to days without hearing any man-made noise.

The first invitation was my choice, this one was not. I ws anxious because Jim was not pleased. Fortunately, the evening with our stranger was short because he went straight to bed. Jim seemed peaceful as he read by the fire. He was in the middle of his fifth consecutive Faulkner novel. The plot's dark intrigue and misdeeds underscored his mistrust of Bracken.

Hadn't he confessed his past alcoholism, his negligent child support? Where would his unwillingness to uphold boundaries end? How many more of our boundaries would we need to forego before we could return to our candle lit bath and comfortable routine?

In the morning, Bracken called his mom and she agreed to send him money so he could return home. For them, the timing was perfect. After ten years of her telling him to not bring his troubles to her, he finally grew up and became independent. Until now. Five days earlier, he had called her from Chico. The next day, she heard about a mountain lion attack on a young man. She had worried for three days, so was glad when he called.

The heavy feeling lifted enough for us to acknowledge the twinkle in Bracken's eye and receive his gift. He unrolled a well-made hammock of many colors, which he had carried around the world. It could live here among the oaks and nestle us in a shady breeze during the hot summer. He noted that his pack would be much lighter.

108

Jim offered to drive him to town, but since Bracken was my responsibility, I assured him that I would complete the deed and not bring him back.

Driving out, I realized what a long thirteen miles he had walked from town. Part of the time he had to carry Agnes in his arms like a baby. His feet were sore because his boots were not broken in.

I told him he might consider scrapping intuition now and then. There was something to be said for planning, or at least looking at maps. He was crazy to set out on an impossibly long hike into wild country on a stormy night in winter. But then, I came around the bend, didn't I?

Bracken said he had trust. He learned from all adventures and now he was glad to be going home to be near his daughters. But first, he'd do some "couch surfing" and visit his cousin in Southern California.

WILD BOAR

We were gazing at meadow grasses tipped gold as the sun rose when I heard a piercing scream. Snorting sows, dozens of piglets and youngsters hustled before us on their way to a muddy, wallowing area below our spring. For hours more than 50 wild pigs sounded like monsters belching, slurping and gnashing their teeth.

Not long after, Jesús hosted a feast and we met his hunting buddy, Norm. When he was 14 years old, Norm began learning about guns from older hunters. He became an expert tracker and developed ethics: eat what you kill, never leave a wounded animal even if you have to chase it up and down steep ravines and through jungles of brush and brambles. He observes safety precautions for his dogs.

110

Norm's main challenge is making the clean, perfect shot. If he doesn't have the opportunity to aim for the head or neck and kill with one shot, he doesn't shoot. Except once: he inadvertently slid down a ravine and came face to face with a boar. The 300 pounder lowered his bristly head with razor sharp tusks that can slice through bullet-proof vests. Terrified and out of breath, Norm shot quickly. The beast came at him while his dogs tackled on three sides. It took multiple close-range shots before the boar died. The dogs were ok.

Norm's policy is to not shoot sows. He accidentally killed a pregnant sow once and immediately performed a C-section to save two piglets. He blew their nostrils out, gave them CPR, took them home to a warm bed. Two hours later, he returned to the dead sow and carried her home for butchering.

A rancher hired Norm to kill all the pigs on his property. After the boss left, Norm used his dogs to round up and capture the sows. He managed to tape shut the jaws, bind the feet, and clean the wounds inflicted by his dogs. He hauled each one out and exported them to more northern wild lands.

Norm's most memorable hunt was for The Phantom. Easily recognizable because of a twisted foot, this giant boar had been tracked by Norm and his friends for 20 years. By chance, the dogs found the famous beast and chased him into a vulnerable position. After all those years roaming the hills and outwitting hunters, with one shot The Phantom was gone, became sausage.

Norm says he has loved hunting because he was hooked on adrenaline, an acutely sharpened appreciation for being alive, and a sense of achievement. These last years, Norm has also been proud of his photographic shots as he continues to learn the ways of wild animals, the lay of the land, the smell of forests and streams. Sometimes, he's out there all night. With or without a moon. In all seasons.

BONFIRES

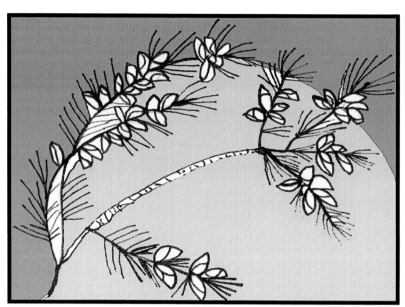

During the rainy season, ranchers clear old brush, unhealthy trees and thickets of firs. This is necessary for the health of oaks and other large trees. Firs quickly proliferate. I counted more than 50 new "conelettes" on one twig. Each mature, pollinated female cone releases 25-30 seeds. Although many of these are eaten by birds and animals, hundreds of fir seedlings sprout. With decreased fir expansion, meadow grassses have sunlight and room to flourish. Mice, voles, rabbits, hawks, deer and other creatures in the food chain have plenty to eat.

Jim's love of the land and passion for stewardship propels him to tromp through meadows and forests with loppers and chain saw. Sometimes he pulls up 600 small seedlings in an afternoon. Or he thins roadside thickets and lashes a dozen or more ten-foot firs to the back bumper of the truck. Sometimes I lie on the sleigh of plush, soft boughs and ride up to our fire pit.

Coals from these fires can be so hot that a heavy rain does not extinguish them. They remain alive all night; the next morning, we bury russet potatoes. Half an hour later, we fish for black, charred *mickies* with a pitchfork. The crunchy, black crust cools off quickly.

112

After adding butter, salt and pepper to each half, we scoop out the steaming, soft insides. The more burned on the outside, the tastier on the inside.

With friends from the city, we prepare a country stew. The cast iron pot is filled with rutabagas, yams, leeks, garlic, rosemary, thyme, salt collected from the sea, chuck roast and red wine. We expect it to simmer slowly all night in hot ashes and coals, and imagine feasting on the hearty, tender *ragout* throughout the next day.

In the morning, we gallop toward the fire pit, carefully excavate the pot and brush ashes away from the top. We lift the lid, peer inside. Nothing. Not a scrap, not an iota of moisture, no messy pan, no lump of charcoal. Stewed, reduced, dehydrated, toasted, burned to a crisp, disintegrated. The scoured, unbelievably empty pot strikes us as the funniest dinner party ever. For the rest of the visit, we eat boxed food from the store.

Jesús and Pat's bonfire parties are much more successful. Wild pig in homemade chili sauce stews all day. Families gather around cooking fires with cauldrons so large that a man stirs them with a tree trunk. Barbecued oysters, chicharrones, tamales, salsa and rice, limes and cucumbers, hot punch simmered with tropical fruit: a feast. After dinner, the children have their own small fire, where they toast marshmellows.

We sit around a 15-foot pile of flaming logs. Two visiting ten-year old girls from the city cheer, chant and clap to the tune of crackling sparks. A four year old exclaims "Ahhh, the parade is beginning!" as orange specks swirl and fly up through the veil of falling mist.

A foggy, fuzzy glow around the full moon is echoed in a large ring of light. Smoky air spiced with pine needles mingles with the scents of rain-soaked, spongy earth.

ADOPTIONS

At last night's bonfire, the guests from the city clustered around an old-timer as he described the abandoned newborn lamb found in a boggy pasture. He and his wife surrendered to caring for the baby in their kitchen. Bottle feeding every four hours, outdoor potty breaks and mishaps caused by a rambunctious new creature were offset by its tenacity and sweetness. Speaking of the lamb, the rancher shook his head, his enormous beard glinting from the orange fire, and exclaimed repeatedly, "SUCH a will to live! A fierce will to live!"

This morning, we took the two girls, who are adopted, to visit the lamb. One solemnly asked, "Why did the ewe walk away from her first baby?" --Maybe she was distracted as she meandered off to give birth to the second lamb. As she heard the second baby's cry, she bonded with it. Later, she didn't recognize the first lamb's cry and refused to accept it. No comforting answers.

There was no time to remain disturbed. The fluffy, frisky, gamboling, curious youngster nudged the girls. They were enchanted as they took turns letting it suck their fingers with its soft tongue.

114

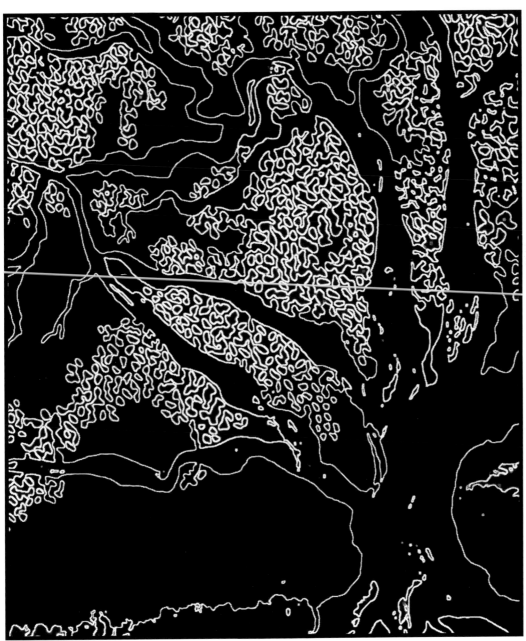

115

Jim's Exit Plans

I just learned you don't have to be embalmed by law. I don't want to be.
I used to think I'd be in a casket,
thought it would slide down a declivity and
I'd have to wait for a shift in tectonic plates
before I'd be liberated.

Ideally, I want to be put in the ground
so I can get back into circulation.
Plant a tree on top of me.

If I don't have to be put in a casket,
put my body in a winding cloth and
if I don't have to have a winding cloth,
put me buck naked into the earth.
Don't put in any good shoes or specs
or anything else.

No, I don't want to give disintegration a jump start
with cremation. I'm afraid I would
blow away and be dispersed.
I want to be fertilizer for the living.

When I learned my molecules
are recycled from the stars, grass, dirt, water,
I figured I'd want to go back home as soon as possibile.

I'd like to push up a few trees
before sliding into the subduction zone.
What's a few thousand years
in the big scheme?

Birds

Red-tail hawks,

stellar jays imitate
the red-tails' hunting cries,

acorn woodpeckers chase,
swipe,
harass
jays in mid-air,

pileated woodpeckers
peck bongo drum style,

dozens of small, rosy finches
dart in and out of the oaks,

grouse hide in bushes,
their calls low and muffled,

starlings fly away so fast
they seem have four wings.

Sparrows, vultures,
towhees, golden eagles,
hummingbirds, great-horned owls,
juncos, blue herons,
wrens, Canada geese,

red-shafted flickers.

Saw-whet owls: boop boop
boop boop monotone boop,

pigmy owls softly converse
in the gloaming and at dawn,

wild turkeys have been around 11 million years,

one robin pulls out
12 worms in five minutes,

irridescent blue bunting lazuli flits,

12 ravens "whomp, whomp" at sunset:
their powerful wings reflect orange
instead of shiny, blue-black.

One by one, band-tailed pigeons
quietly land on the oak branch lit by early morning sun;
a dozen or more line up side by side,
soak up warmth for ten minutes.
Suddenly,
at some unknown signal,
they take off with a simultaneous
thundering flap,
and fly up into the day.

a whisper, a faint stirring, a breeze, a wake-up refreshening; away down the valleys roar around us with a million 3-inch long leaves tapered at each end and while orange gold say ... envelop us with ... sideways around us and beyond.... Then, complete calm.

Rancho Report: January 2010

Wild Plum Café, looking back and forward, storm, quail

Since you have heard me complain about roughing it, I want you to know that we are much more comfortable than before. Projects are ongoing, the rhythm of the days is harmonious and Jim continues to make me laugh. I am learning to live with uncertainty the way I have become accustomed to rattlers. Last night I dreamed I ran around the meadow swiftly, with ease. I was surprised but not frightened to discover 70 rattlers. (I am almost 70.) I looked carefully. Stretched out, in curvy zig zags, coiled, resting or slithering--they were not horrifying.

But feeling content is not as much fun to write about. This may be the last letter. Your interest in the Rancho Reports has prompted me to write *Wild Plum Café,* which is almost finished. I am pondering the ending. Before writing about the fire that raged through our lives, I had a lurch in my stomach whenever I thought about it. Now it is something that happened, an event that made these adventures possible. We can't imagine living anywhere else. Learning about this niche in the natural world excites us.

Our recent visit to grandchildren triggered overwhelming nostalgia. On Sunday morning, we decided to not watch *The Incredible Hulk* on TV. Within moments, instead of arguing, the four and six year old boys were reading books. Even the 18-month sister was turning pages in her pop-up book. I was thrilled, but aware of layers of personal history, chords of emotions.

The tour of their Montessori school reminded me of years in my classroom where children discovered talents, learned self control and enjoyed being part of a group. Yesterday, I once again touched beautifully made wooden equipment in an orderly environment: map puzzles with small knobs for picking up each piece, the tray with a juicer, cutting board and knife for cutting oranges, math bead sets for understanding tens, hundreds, thousands, the small broom and dust pan on hooks.

At their home, another memory bank lit up. While folding toddler socks and shirts, a kalaidoscope of

121

past decades: joyful, tender, intense experiences of mothering punctuated by challenges. Bent over the washing machine, time collapsed, manifested in heavy breathing and tears. I don't wish to return to any previous phase of life, but regret how quickly time passes. Dementia and decrepitude lurk. The pen in my hand will shake and I may not dare face the blank page. Our years in these hills teeming with wild life will be soon be over. In another wink, my dance will be done. The tango of desire and acceptance, fear of the unknown and awareness of the moment will rest.

Ecological, social, political problems are daunting. I used to expend a great deal of energy to help make big changes. Now it is enough to live in an earth-friendly manner. Jim is glad to care for meadows and forests. He hopes to die with his backpack on and loppers in his hand.

This morning the gnarled branches and enormous oak trunks swayed gently in fierce wind and horizontal sheets of rain. Curled up on the bed, the cats began to purr as soon as my hand neared them. The tough flexibility of old trees and the sensuous awareness of cats simmer in my psyche while I spread out 70 dried bean pods on the table. I am overdue for sorting and saving seeds for next season's planting.

Rain has subsided and a dozen plump quail are pecking for insects. Their glossy, tan and black feather patterns make them almost invisible on the brown pathway. Usually, they scare instantly. Their cries of alarm, loud flapping wings, their necks stretched out on the runway before taking off make me laugh. They remind me of how I felt when I first came here.

Thank you for continuing to write, call and visit.

Love,
Gretchen and Jim

Without knowing why, we packed my dad's bowling ball in the U-Haul trailer. Jim and Dave Carr created our mascot, who guides visitors on the unmarked dirt road.

WILD PLUM PHOTOS

Jim and I manage to push and scoot the 2,500 gallon-tank to the levelled spot. I think the tank will escape and roll down the hill, but Jim has it under control.

He has put in pipes to carry the water downhill to our camp, where I will enjoy using it for cooking, showers and mini-gardens.

A local commercial delivery truck will fill the tank this first summer. By next summer, Jim will have installed the water collection and pumping systems down at the spring.

Each morning, I fill the two-gallon shower bags that warm in the sun. When the temperature is just right, which depends on the sun's position and the day's weather, we stop work, hoist the bag with a crude pulley, fasten the rope and *then* have a shower.

Upper right: Jim's brother, Roger, sings, dances and works on the yurt's piers.

The laptop is powered by an inverter in the truck battery. We receive messages through the underground phone line, our one amenity.

Twenty-four piers are attached to the mainbeams of the yurt's subflooring.

Roger inspects the first 2"x 8" cross beam.

Upper right: Jerry Taylor pounds tongue and groove floor boards.

While working, one of the guys misses the nail and mars the board. He signs his name on the floor, which we preserve under the final coat of polyeurythane.

In the center of the floor, Jim attaches the compass made from a 24-foot board. He uses it to mark the circumference of the yurt floor.

Lower right: the lattice wall structure with doors in place. Roof rafters are positioned with the plexi-glass dome frame.

Later, we learn that light through the dome makes our round, 400 square-foot space feel cheerful even on gray days. Moonlight is romantic, lightning storms dramatic.

Jim and Dave Carr put up the rafters.

Hoisting the heavy roofing material through the dome hole requires ingenuity. After sleeping on the problem, they painstakingly winch the folded insulation and roofing through the hole with a come-along.

In a circle, starting at one o'clock: Dave Carr, Rebecca Rollins, Jerry Taylor, Gretchen and Jim.

We construct the yurt on the knoll, camp and dine in the Wild Plum Café.

The morning sun warms the yurt so that on fall and winter days, we usually don't light a fire until mid-afternoon.

Right: I did not insert the rays of light with Photoshop. I'm not sure how they got there.

I prefer to hang laundry to the tune of cicadas and bird songs rather than stay at the laundromat while machines whirr and spin.

The garden provides never ending entertainment. I look forward to germinating and sprouting seeds, gently tucking seedlings with tangles of delicate roots into the earth, feeling and smelling warm, moist soil, encouraging worms with mulch. Discovering beneficial insects, planting quickly growing, short-rooted salad greens beneath large, leafy broccoli, planning for other mutually beneficial plant companions and crop rotation enhance our appreciation of the harvest. Saving seeds, weeding, removing old plants, digging after spring rains to prepare new beds, feeling the whirly flutter of a humming bird in morning sun are part of the fun.

When I am blue, have the blahs, or if I'm hungry, I head for the garden. A sunlit poppy petal, a twisting, climbing bean tendril, a cluster of mint shimmering with butterflies capture my attention. I never know what small surprise awaits.

The quilt, a gift made from old levis by Marla Collins, keeps us cozy in winter and hangs on the wall as art in the summer. Other seasons, it hangs on a dowel and becomes a door that provides insulation and privacy for guests.

Fabrics given by friends who travel cover the criss-cross lattice. Flavors from Africa, Japan, Mexico, Ecuador, Indonesia, Guatemala, and India are part of the entertainment.

Not shown: sunshine streaming through the dome. It spotlights the dog, cats and the hair they shed, unwashed dishes, clumps of dirt on the floor. And more.

Below: my dad's dial telephone is fascinating to Merlín and Sito. They look forward to using it when they call home.

Jim horses around while plumbing the sink, which we purchased from Recycle Town for $10. The plywood counter's blue and white boat paint is decorated with phases of the moon cut out from my art card scraps.

Note the curve of light at the top. As the sun progresses through the day, different parts of the interior are lit up.

140

Jim's shop inside the cargo container: shelves hold tools, rusty washers, horseshoes and toys unearthed while he dug trenches and holes. Sandpapers, tapes, wrenches, pliers, screwdrivers and levels are organized. Next to 62 small drawers, six kinds of tape measures, a "Boo!" candywrapper adorns the shelf. He makes room for mirrors, artwork and wine bottles for a future bottle wall like the one in Palmer Canyon.

Although space is limited, Jim stores large boxes of parts. I was going to describe the Ranchers' Rule, but he says this is the Universal Rule: As soon as you throw a part away, you will need it.

141

Jungle Gym Days: Merlín, Sito and Jim rig up a rope swing and trapeze. The kids perform daring tricks and take 500 action photos of each other. We could make an entire book on this day alone.

Below: Sito's shrewd chess strategies keeep us on our toes, but Canasta with partners is our favorite game. Before her turn, Merlín never tires of chanting, "Give me something good!"

I don't have a photo of our rainy day bowling alley. We take turns with a soccer ball that crashes into creatively constructed four-foot high towers of toilet paper rolls.

Although Merlín and Sito had named the kittens Midnight and Starfire, we talk to them with nicknames: Gray Man, Rat Man, Stretch, Slinky, Snodgrass, Fang, Lizard Breath, Gilmore, Fuzzmore, Joy Boys, Nancy Boys, McGill, Jiffy Pop, Gato, Miguel, Bozo, Bolivar, Captain Midnight, Bohunkus.

I wish we had photos of Merlín making "Early Grey" tea and Sito cooking and serving us golden brown *quesadillas*.

The plum is one of the earliest trees to blossom. Starting with the first few flowers, wild bees come from hidden winter hives and begin collecting the season's nectar.

On Valentine's Day, Jim brings me a truck load of compost as a romantic gift. Under the plum's snowy petals, the black mound promises a robust summer garden. We will enjoy flowers, fruit and fresh vegetables with friends in the Wild Plum Café.

Gretchen Butler is an artist and gardener in rural Northern California. She lives with her husband and two cats.